UNIQUELY
YOU

T0282135

UNIQUELY
YOU

EXPLORING YOUR CHILD'S
EXTRAORDINARILY DISTINCTIVE DESIGN

SALLY CLARKSON & NATHAN CLARKSON

MOODY PUBLISHERS
CHICAGO

Published in association with the literary agency: The Bindery Agency.

Edited by Amanda Cleary Eastep
Interior and cover design: Kaylee Lockenour Dunn
Cover photo of happy children copyright © 2024 by Storyblocks (SBI-300912934). All rights reserved.

ISBN: 978-0-8024-3278-0

Originally delivered by fleets of horse-drawn wagons, the affordable paperbacks from D. L. Moody's publishing house resourced the church and served everyday people. Now, after more than 125 years of publishing and ministry, Moody Publishers' mission remains the same—even if our delivery systems have changed a bit. For more information on other books (and resources) created from a biblical perspective, go to www.moodypublishers.com or write to:

Moody Publishers
820 N. LaSalle Boulevard
Chicago, IL 60610

1 3 5 7 9 10 8 6 4 2

Printed in the United States of America

To my son Nathan, who is every bit as unique as I am. —Sally

To my mom, who is every bit as unique as I am. —Nathan

Contents

Welcome to My World: Sally

The memory is as fresh to me now as ever. My family had taken their place in a long, uncomfortable wooden pew in our old mission-style church in the heart of Albuquerque, New Mexico. Intricately carved beams covered the ceiling and created a sort of spiritual shelter above us. I am quite sure that in my restless body, I had studied, counted, and pondered each beam meticulously to entertain myself through the long services.

Often, out of nervousness or boredom or maybe just some anxious thoughts, I would bounce my leg up and down in a frenetic rhythm, totally unselfconscious that I was jiggling myself and the others in our row. It might have been acceptable when I was a small child, but now as a preteen, it was more conspicuous. My mother would turn to me with a familiar glance and nearly imperceptible shake of her head. Each time, she would reach over and softly squeeze my shoulder as if to say, "Stop it! You are shaking the whole row of people."

I wasn't *trying* to be disruptive. I didn't even know I was doing it—my wiggles and leg bouncing just burst forth as a natural expression of what was bubbling up from inside. It was an unintentional expression of all my energy, ideas, and thoughts. Yet, at this point, a little dread would come upon me. And so, I would feel corrected, again, *for just being myself.*

Sometimes, I would look at the world and especially people, and spew out a million and one questions. *What do you think about this? Why that? Do you think God is really like the story the preacher talked about at church today? I don't agree with the premise!* And on and on. I wasn't *trying* to be obnoxious, I just thought about everything and wanted the world, truth, and answers to make sense. I never have been able to stop thinking and pondering life.

Once my mother looked at me with deep frustration and said, "Why do you *always* ask so many questions? Why can't you be like other kids and just accept life as it is? Don't you know your constant questions and comments are, at times, irritating?"

I had a growing feeling inside that, in most ways, I was just "too much." And so, I grew up feeling that I was different and that being my true self irritated some people—at the very least, my mother.

Fast-forward forty-five years.

Once again, I was in a church, a much larger one this time. I was sitting next to a wiggly little nine-year-old boy. He was bouncing his leg up and down at the speed of light. His gaze scanned the church where several thousand people were gathered—singing, listening, worshiping. I knew that for this little one—my son—sitting still for an hour was excruciatingly challenging. I reached over and gently tickled his back in a way that pleased him and brought a smile to his face. I mouthed, "Love you!" and smiled at him.

Life had taught me that gentleness and acceptance was a healing influence that this boy and all my children craved. They needed to feel free to be who they were created to be. My whole life I wanted to be accepted as I was, cherished for my irrepressible questions, valued for the curiosity and vibrancy that danced within me. It was from that desire to be understood that I approached each of my children as totally unique and individual from every other person, believing that they would grow stronger and healthier when they were validated as a masterpiece from the hand of God within the context and limitations of their own God-given personalities.

If every person who is ever formed has a unique DNA that translates to different sizes and shapes and eye colors and smiles and hairlines, then perhaps God meant for our personalities to be different by design too. Perhaps our personalities give scope to the full expression of the creative God and give glory and praise to His beautiful design.

The messages in this book are a continuation of a story that began with my earlier book *Different*, which I also wrote with Nathan. In that story, I was able to open up about my journey as a mom, loving and accepting the outside-the-box boy who just didn't fit the mold, learning to see with new eyes the precious soul underneath the roiling ball of uncontainable energy and expression that my son was and is. And Nathan was able to give a window into his own experience of growing up with a smattering of mental issues, from OCD to ADHD, and how our relationship made it possible for him to find his own unique pathway into happiness and wholeness. When we released *Different*, we were unprepared for the amazing reception it would receive from so many parents and kids who had walked their own different pathway together. It was a great privilege to share in their stories and that we are all on a similar journey together.

In *Uniquely You*, Nathan and I want to invite you further into the story we began with *Different*. In this book, it is our hope that we can provide a strategic framework within which you can approach each of your children, no matter their strengths and weaknesses, their individual personality traits, and the things they cherish. Every child is unique, deserves to be seen on their own merits, and to be loved in their particularity. In *Uniquely You*, Nathan and I will open up nine dimensions of delving into your child's individual artistry, helping you to see and affirm them where they are and draw them into their best selves.

There are *three principles* that will guide you through the journey in this book: to learn how to *accept, affirm,* and *delight* in your children.

To *accept* your child is a radical act. It is learning how to see them with unvarnished eyes—not imagining them as you want them to be or trying to fit them into a particular mold, but genuinely seeing what they are in their capacities and limitations, their hopes and fears. This is the first step toward understanding your child as *unique*. Just like you and me, our children are fearfully and wonderfully made by God in a way that is particular to them and to the story they will tell with their lives. If we spend our time trying to change our children into something they are not, not only will we not succeed, but they will ultimately feel rejected and like failures. Our first step is to learn how to see with honest eyes, and only in this do we set up ourselves—and our children—for a sustainable pathway together.

To *affirm* our children is to go a step further and to say to them, "I see your individual expression, and it is good. Who you are is valuable and worthwhile. I'm glad you are the way you are." This step requires a willingness to use words of life and to make them a central part of your relationship with your child. You go beyond simply acknowledging in a neutral sense what their unique makeup is; instead, you make them feel that what they *are* is acceptable and they are capable of being integrated into the community of your family. You, as a mom, are the first to affirm your child's underlying goodness in this way.

Finally, to *delight* in your child is a step that happens in your own heart. Delight is perhaps the hardest because there will undoubtedly be those days where the differences between you and your child will simply feel insurmountable, and you will wonder how you can find your way forward with them. But unconditional love paves the pathway to delight, where we learn to celebrate our precious child. This kind of acceptance is always a choice, and it is a habit we develop in ourselves as parents. It expresses truthfulness even if we don't always feel the emotions of love and delight, but only if we practice an attitude of kindness and love in our hearts first. Only then can delight blossom and overflow into the lives of each of our children.

To accept, affirm, and delight in your child as *unique* is no small feat, and in this book, Nathan and I want to provide meaningful steps into that process.

We want to both encourage and help parents and families discover the beautiful and unique design of all of us. Each chapter will begin with a "letter" offering stories that relate to what will be explored in that chapter. These letters are composites that represent the countless questions we have received over the years from parents just like you. We hope that in these letters you will find comfort in knowing you are not alone in your questions and difficulties. Following each letter, you'll read my response, and then Nathan's, offering insight into these varied experiences.

We hope that as you join us, you will begin to feel your own parenting muscles strengthened for the way ahead.

Welcome to My World: Nathan

I remember asking my mom on a whim if she'd ever be interested in writing a book with me—a book about our story. The story of me, a kid struggling through life with mental illness and a plethora of learning disabilities, and her, a mom learning how to love and raise that kid. She loved the idea, and we pitched the book, *Different*, to a publisher who agreed to give the book a shot. We didn't expect it to go that far, given that it was a book of personal stories and reflections on a niche issue. We just hoped it would encourage the few people who might pick it up and read our story. Then just a year and a half later, on the day of the book's release, we found ourselves being interviewed on NBC's *Today* show. In the following days, the book became a national Publishers Weekly bestseller. We were shocked! We didn't totally understand why our collection of personal stories around a very specific subject seemed to resonate the way it did with so many.

But over the years, we have received thousands of messages from parents and children alike from around the world, telling us their stories and how they connected to our story of discovering, accepting, and ultimately celebrating the unique ways God had created me. It's become increasingly obvious to us that this topic of every child being unique while living in a world that expects and demands conformity is not only a relevant one to continue exploring, but one that strikes at the heart of how God designed us to live our lives.

God created every one of us brilliantly unique in a multitude of ways. But so often in modern culture, we are made to feel that these "uniquenesses" are bad, annoying, or unwanted; that the outside-the-box aspects of ourselves have no place in the world and are in need of "fixing" or even eliminating. This so-called fixing doesn't work, and it actually goes against God's design for how He wants the world to look and who He has called us to be. Trying to force children into a societal mold doesn't create better kids, it breaks them. For children to grow up to be all that God has intended, their unique design must not only be fostered but celebrated, accepted, and loved.

I was a unique kid who felt the daily pain of a world trying to fit me inside a box that I was never going to fit. But I had parents who listened to God, appreciated His unique design for me, and created a space in our home where I could grow freely into the person God created me to be, to tell the story He had created me to tell.

In our first book, we told our story, one about my specific uniquenesses that came in the form of mental illness and learning disabilities. But a child's uniqueness will appear in a myriad of ways. While the last book focused on one small section of how I was unique, in this book we want to explore the gamut of ways every child is different. We want to continue this conversation to help you examine and understand *your* and *your child's* story. In the coming pages, we look at the main ways every child is created uniquely and how to deal with those uniquenesses in a lifegiving way. Ultimately, we hope to offer inspiration and practical advice for how to celebrate and cultivate these differences in your child so they can flourish inside their very own story.

At the end of each chapter, you'll find a section designed to help you and your family do this together. We recommend reading a chapter each week and going through these family discussion questions together to bring about greater connection, understanding, and joy.

INSIST ON YOURSELF; NEVER IMITATE.

RALPH WALDO EMERSON

CHAPTER ONE

Fearfully and Wonderfully Made

Dear Sally and Nathan,

We are loving parents who desire the best for our three amazing children. When we began our parenting journey, we read every book and resource available at the time. These books spoke with authority on the best methods and formulas for parents. We took to heart what they had to say and felt prepared with a well-defined strategy planned out. But now, seven years into parenthood, we are suddenly feeling lost and overwhelmed. The singular advice and specific methods found in these books seem inadequate to address all the individual needs of our three very different children. What works for one, doesn't work for the other. We want to give our children what they need, but it seems there is no one method that works for all of them when it comes to our parenting. This has gotten us to a place where we feel lost, tired, and a bit hopeless in our ability to parent our children in a cohesive way. We love all of them and just need some insight in how to proceed and what direction we should walk with them.

—Louise

From Sally:

Thirty years ago, I was exhausted to my toes.

A respiratory virus had slowly moved viciously through our family, leaving us tired and ragged. Every night had left me caring for a different child and the sleeplessness had left me listless and drained. Somehow, three-year-old Nathan had avoided the dreaded plague, and for a moment, I believed against hope that all might be well, until, suddenly, he started to cough.

As the illness descended upon Nathan, my husband, Clay, offered to take the other kids out to church. Fatigued, I nonetheless stayed home with Nathan to keep him company and see him through the illness on my own. I felt insufficient to the task, introverted, and just wanting to retreat into my own quiet solitude for a moment of respite.

As I sat down on the couch, Nathan came bounding in with a smile and sat next to me. Pressing down the exhaustion, I turned to him and asked him what he wanted to do.

"Let's talk!" he proclaimed, confidently.

And for the next forty-five minutes, that is precisely what we did. I entered into every little dimension of his universe: from his observations and interests to his perspectives on other children, to his cherished delights and genuine concerns. I listened attentively, giving him dedicated eye contact and rubbing his back gently while he chattered on. Soon, the busy line of conversation trickled as he began to grow tired. As his energy slipped away, he looked at me with earnest and said, "I feel so close to you, Mama. I wish we could spend more time talking together. I just have lots of things to say! Thank you for listening to me."

With those words, my mama heart melted, and I saw, perhaps for the first time, the real Nathan underneath the incessant wiggles and disruption. I saw, as if in an epiphany, the truth about Nathan. He is a verbal processor. For Nathan, what he still desires more than anything is to be heard, to be allowed to speak his thoughts in relationship with those whom he most loves. I realized in that moment that I was his confidant, and that in opening up to me, he was allowing me to access a genuine and sincere part of his personality.

I thought of how some of his teachers told me with exasperation that he constantly needed to be hushed; and I realized just how counterproductive and wrong that attitude was. They presumed he was rebellious and attempted to subdue something that was never meant to be suppressed in him. It was to Nathan's glory, and essentially to God's, for him to be able to communicate and open up about the world of words and ideas constantly bouncing around in his head—especially at three years old! I saw, in an instant, that this is who Nathan was, and if I was to truly love him, I needed to make space to hear his words and to affirm them. There would always be time for training, which we did on a continual basis, and helping him to learn to listen to others, but I needed to see that his bursting heart was good.

This is a crucial part of our responsibility as parents: to accept the reality that each child is made uniquely with their own capacities, personalities, interests, strengths, and weaknesses. Our children are their own special stories, books waiting to be opened up and read with interest. You and I as parents are the readers, the ones who might take the time to dive deep into the whole story of their creative individuality. The book of every child is its own genre, and each child has different "characters" that make up their inner world. In truth, we all are our own stories waiting for others to read us. Just as it delights you and me when someone takes the time to understand our inner workings, so too will your children come to life when you delve into their special narratives.

To achieve this insight requires a special investment of time and energy on our part, a willingness to develop habits of observation, and the patience to allow those aspects of our children to emerge so that we can engage with them in a meaningful way. It is understandable that we often feel tired and simply want to get on with our lives; and yet if we don't take the time to understand, to study and learn each child's "bent," we are inviting more conflict and misunderstanding in the future. The effort we develop in gaining a vision for the uniqueness of our children will in time pay dividends, drawing them closer to us, and allowing us to be set up for success in how we help them be the best version of themselves.

I won't lie to you: learning the inner workings of your child has been a lifetime project and has stretched me more than I could ever have imagined. And yet the process has given me a depth of insight and compassion, not only for my children but also for other people in my life as well.

To do this work in an effective manner, you will need to develop your own techniques for drawing out these aspects. For instance, two of my children are extroverts, and two of them are introverts. I had to take a different approach with my introverts because they weren't as vocal about their desires; and yet they were just as eager to open up to me and share their thoughts and feelings. I learned that, for them, it was necessary to sequester them in their own individual time and space so that they feel comfortable opening up. Not only is it acceptable to manage each child's needs according to their particular makeup; it was necessary for a whole and healthy relationship with each child.

There is no formula for discovering the dimensions of each of your precious ones; it is a long-term process of trial and error. But the more you listen and observe, letting them communicate themselves to you in their own way, the more you will become an expert in understanding each of your children. You will become a trusted interpreter of them, helping them understand themselves, their family members, and the world around them in a way that strengthens them and helps them thrive.

Every child is designed uniquely by God, and He has entrusted you with His special creations. Over time, we can move away from seeking to mold our children into our own image so they're easier to manage, and instead, learn to see them as unique, creative expressions of God's design. They are fearfully and wonderfully made by Him (Psalm 139:14)! Through patience and commitment, we will eventually reap a harvest. Today, I encourage you to begin the journey of discovering the individual wonders of each one.

From Nathan:

I remember lying stomach-down on the floor as a six-year-old poring over the beautiful pages of the book in front of me. My mother sat next to me pointing out details of the wonderfully drawn artwork that covered its shiny paper. The book was called *Noah's Ark* and was a giant collection of pages filled with a master artist's rendering of nature, animals, and creation in all its glory.

I gazed wide-eyed at the wonders of God's beautiful creation reflected in the paintings of lions, tigers, bears, deer, eagles, lizards, and more. But my mom had shown me this book, not for a random moment of novelty, but instead intentionally with a message to share and a lesson to impart. She knew that recently I had been struggling, even at six years old, with getting in trouble, keeping up with schoolwork, and feeling like I was "too much." So, she pulled out the giant book, almost as big as my little body, set it on the floor, and bid me to come and look at it with her.

As we explored the enchanting pictures, she made a point to

underline the obvious, showing the vast diversity of creativity God had expressed when making the natural world, before turning to me and saying, "Nathan, do you see how different and unique God has made all the plants and animals in nature? How each one is so different, but so beautiful as they serve a unique purpose for which they were created?"

"Yeth," I replied, with my six-year-old lisp, looking up at her with innocent and trusting eyes.

"Well, in the same way, God created you unique. And every single way that you might feel different is actually an intentional design by God for the story He has for you to tell."

Every painting was stunning—different colored animals with different designs. Some flew, some swam, some crawled; all unique and made for their own story in God's creation. While I perhaps couldn't grasp the gravity of the message she was sharing that day, the truth was planted somewhere deep in my soul. Many times throughout the years, as I struggled with mental illness, learning disabilities, and an outside-the-box personality, my mom would, in some way, utter those words again: "You were intentionally created unique, and that's a wonderful and beautiful thing." That seed she planted would be watered by her loving words, so that now, almost three decades later, that truth has taken root so deeply in my heart and psyche that it guides, strengthens, and empowers me.

Sometimes, when I'm back in the family home, I hunt through our vast library to find that old book—its pages well-worn and the fingerprints evidence of my childhood fascination—to remind myself of the beautiful truth my mother shared with me all those years ago. Even now, I can be tempted to believe that the things that are different about me are deficiencies and the unique aspects of my personhood are curses. But as I pore over those still-beautiful pages, I am reminded of the God to whom my mother introduced me—the God who is a grand and wonderful artist; who made endless colors, countless species, and a never-ending world of diverse beauty. That same God made me unique in my own right; and that's a wonderful and beautiful thing.

In Scripture, the psalmist writes:

For you created my inmost being;
you knit me together in my mother's womb.
I praise you because I am fearfully and wonderfully made;
your works are wonderful,
I know that full well. (Psalm 139:13–14)

This gives us an insight into God's original design for the world, and for us, one where each of us was created intentionally and carefully with unique skills, longings, abilities, minds, and hearts. But unfortunately, today's culture has drifted further and further away from God's original plan for who we are and who we were created to be. Now we live in a world that demands conformity, one that tries to take all the unique and beautiful things about us and shove them into a mold that will better fit standardized testing, predictable behavior, and "normal lives."

In the 2018 study "Feeling Special, Feeling Happy,"[1] researchers found that satisfaction with one's uniqueness resulted in more authentic living, and more authentic living correlated to much higher rates of happiness. This study points to the fact that every child has been wired to accept and embrace the things that make them unique, and the science points to the reality that if parents help foster that in the hearts of their children, their children will experience more happiness with both their individual lives and individual selves. This, in turn, will ultimately enable them to live freely and healthily into the story that God has for them.

But the unfortunate thing is that this world seems bent on working against this God-created calling to individuality; the world continues to do this even though it doesn't actually work to bring children future success. Multiple studies have shown over and over again that standardized testing, aside from its questionable ethics of fairness, is a poor metric at predicting a child's future success, and only measures a child's ability to take tests well and memorize meaningless facts they almost immediately forget.[2] It does nothing to measure long-term success in life. But we keep doing it. Why?

Through peer pressure, strict grading systems, standardized testing, and social coercion, modern culture has a vested interest in shaving down and eliminating the things that make us and our kids unique. These things force us into quantifiable lumps that think, speak, and act alike as groups of carbon-copy people who are easier to control, guide, and sum up, rather than collections of uniquely thinking, acting individuals. What culture offers in exchange for the dissolution of our own uniqueness is comfort and perceived safety; it's easier to go with the flow and quiet the things about us that don't fit in. To pursue the career you feel you're supposed to, to find the kind of spouse you're expected to, to live the life you're pressured into. But it's not more beautiful, and it's not how we were created to live.

Psychologist Carl Jung said, "The self as the essence of individuality is the unitemporal and unique; as an archetypal symbol it is a God-image and therefore universal and eternal."[3] In other words, our being made in the image of a unique, outside-the-box, and diversely creative God who doesn't fit the bounds that man has so often tried to put Him in, means we too are made, not as a "grouping," but instead as entirely unparalleled creations with purposes and stories unique to only ourselves. To believe this about ourselves and to impart this to our children will bring a freedom that God designed us to live inside of.

The desire of culture to force us into bland conformity and to rid us of our individually created minds and hearts is nothing new. Some of the greatest thinkers, artists, and inventors throughout history faced intense pushback while living into their unique callings and personhood. Thank goodness they did, as the world is a better place for it.

Of course, every unique attribute we or our kids possess comes with its own unique difficulties. But these difficulties are evidence that every child needs specialized and tailored love and guidance to bring about more intentionally guided freedom, not pressure and conformity that often brings about oppression.

Early on in my life it was clear that I had major mental illness (OCD) and learning disabilities (ADHD, dyslexia). While those were important for my parents to pay attention to, address, and help me with, they instead focused their energy on my strengths, giftings, and passions, not on the areas I struggled with. My mom and dad took note that from a young age, I had a natural ability for creativity, performance, and storytelling—spending hours writing my own scripts and novels, dressing up and playing pretend, and dreaming up detailed imaginary worlds. So instead of forcing me to excel at things I was never made for (like math, spelling, and grammar), they leaned into who God had created me to be as evidenced by my own natural passions and abilities. Of course they helped me in the places I needed assistance, but they celebrated the areas I naturally excelled at, never making me feel "less than" for being the person God had created me to be.

Even when teachers, friends, and "professionals" told my parents I needed to be more disciplined (which veered away from my creative pursuits) or put pressure on me to fit in, I have been able to live a life of freely and wisely following the path God had for me because of the decision my mom and dad made in faith. As an adult, I have spent the last decade working as an actor, author, and filmmaker and every day pursuing my calling; and I can use my gifting and passions, which might never have been possible if my parents had tried to subdue rather than celebrate my unique makeup.

My parents, knowing God, wrapped their entire philosophy of parenting around the truth found in Psalm 139 that their children were "fearfully and wonderfully made," so that even with all my uniquenesses—even the ones that were hard and required patience and grace—they were to be celebrated and cultivated.

But I wasn't the only unique child in our family. I was the third of four children who, like me, were also created with their own unique and beautiful designs, each requiring and receiving the same celebration and cultivation I enjoyed. We were not compared to each other or expected to be like each other. We were encouraged to live into the unique and glorious designs in which we had been created.

The oldest, Sarah, is quiet, graceful, and poetic. Creating worlds of beauty in her mind, she shares and expresses these thoughts with thousands of readers through books filled with prose and deeply felt observations about story, life, and faith. Now she has branched out with her own stories of her beautiful children in her lifegiving and loving home.

Joel, the oldest boy, is our absent-minded professor, who lives in the mental world of an artist. As a composer and fiction writer, his thoughtful reflections on the deep and beautiful parts of life are expressed through his complex and gorgeous musical compositions and imaginative stories.

I am the youngest boy—an outside-the-box lover of thought, story, truth, and ideas that I bring to life with laughter, teasing, and jokes, expressed in my writing and performance. My desire to tell stories grew into a life of acting in a variety of places, and in writing, making movies, books, and podcasts.

Joy, the youngest, is a tenacious and driven soul, dedicated to both learning and teaching those around her the wonders of truth and beauty, all with a wink and pithy remark on her podcasts, in her books, and in classrooms, having fought through the ranks of higher education.

Each of us is so different, but each of us was created uniquely and wonderfully for and by God. God has created each of us—you, me, your kids, everyone—with the care of a master artist, with the intention of a passionate storyteller, with the expertise of a skilled programmer, and with the care of a loving parent. So often we forget the majesty with which we were created; but having been created in the very image of God Himself, we must remember just how uniquely beautiful He has made us. God, as the greatest artist, has created each of us with a diverse array of giftings, needs, longings, and abilities. Like the myriad of colors, textures, smells, animals, trees, rocks, plants, and terrains we find in nature, so too has God designed us with even more majesty, beauty, and diversity.

Scripture Reading

For you created my inmost being;
you knit me together in my mother's womb.
I praise you because I am fearfully and wonderfully made;
your works are wonderful,
I know that full well.
My frame was not hidden from you
when I was made in the secret place,

when I was woven together in the depths of the earth.
Your eyes saw my unformed body;
all the days ordained for me were written in your book
before one of them came to be.
How precious to me are your thoughts, God!
How vast is the sum of them!
Were I to count them,
they would outnumber the grains of sand—
when I awake, I am still with you. (Psalm 139:13–18)

FAMILY DISCUSSION QUESTIONS

1. What ways do you see that you are unique from other people?

2. Do you like the feeling of being unique? How does it feel?

3. What are the hardest and best parts of your uniqueness?

4. How do you see that you could use your uniqueness for God and for good?

5. Is it ever hard to deal with others' unique traits? Why?

PERSONALITY IS THE SUPREME
REALIZATION OF THE INNATE
IDIOSYNCRASY OF A LIVING BEING.
IT IS AN ACT OF HIGH COURAGE
FLUNG IN THE FACE OF LIFE, THE
ABSOLUTE AFFIRMATION OF ALL
THAT CONSTITUTES THE INDIVIDUAL,
THE MOST SUCCESSFUL ADAPTATION
TO THE UNIVERSAL CONDITIONS
OF EXISTENCE COUPLED WITH THE
GREATEST POSSIBLE FREEDOM FOR
SELF-DETERMINATION.

CARL JUNG

CHAPTER TWO

Personality Types

Dear Sally and Nathan,

I'm a mom of three very different kids. My husband and I are peaceful and highly responsible, so we naturally tend toward desiring order and peace. We more or less believed our personalities would be passed on to our kids. This has not been the case. Our first child (14, girl) is very much like us: she has high standards, organizational skills, enjoys schedules she can depend on, and avoids conflict. She is what you might call an easy child. Our second child (12, boy) is unique from her, as he is a bit all over the place and absent-minded, but he is gentle and loving. While there was some adjusting to his different ways, he was always willing to learn and grow. Our third child (9, girl) is a whole different story. From the day she came into this world, it was clear she had a personality distinct from the rest of us. She is vocal and argumentative; she is hyperactive and loves to be on the go with as many people as possible. We love her so much and never want her to feel anything but acceptance from us, but it can be such a difficult task integrating her "outside-the-box" ways into a family of introverts, especially when she argues with her siblings, needs a higher amount of attention and activity, and isn't easy to discipline. How do we love her in a way that is both healthy for our family and for her?

—Linda

From Sally:

A couple months ago found me nestled deep into an ancient and beloved leather sofa at the vicarage home of my daughter Sarah. On both sides were three warm little bodies squishing as close to me as possible. Like so many occasions when visiting with my sweet grandchildren, I had a book in hand—in this instance, a beautifully illustrated fairy tale full of daring and hope and delight. As I brought the words to life from the page, my audience of three were uncharacteristically quiet, taking in the charming colors and textures of the exquisitely drawn scenes and losing themselves in the lilt of the rollicking story.

Soon, we turned to the final page. The damsel had been rescued, the dragon slain, and the knight had won the hand of his fair maiden. I closed the cover, and as if on cue, the peaceful space transformed into a whirlwind of motion as my small compatriots sprang into action around me.

The first of the three, the eldest of my grandchildren, twirled into the open space in front of the fireplace, dancing wistfully, and clasping her hands together: "I want to be just like the princess and have everyone like me, especially the handsome knight."

The second, in typical boyish gusto, took a fearsome stance, curling his fingers into dragon-like claws, and roaring out his proclamation: "I'm a dragon and I'm going to find my dragon friends!" He stalked around with a grimace, growling once more for good measure.

At the same instant, the third child grasped the book I had been holding and pulled it close to herself. "Mine!" she proclaimed without any malice, and yet also without any intention of relinquishing her prize.

I laughed and released the book into the care of my youngest grandchild, marveling as I watched each of the children around me manifesting their personalities with such glee and warmth. The eldest, self-aware and sensitive, wanted nothing more than to be seen and admired by her adoring family. The middle child, by contrast, couldn't have cared less about being noticed; he simply wanted to disappear into the enjoyment of his make-believe world. And the youngest expressed her strength and confidence; from the beginning she had been a force of nature equal to the task of her older siblings, fearless and ready to take on the world.

The thing is, they started expressing these ways of being almost from the moment they came out of the womb. Of course, as soon as they were old enough, my wonderful daughter began training them, shaping their wills to trust and obey their parents and to love their siblings. And yet, just as I had with my children, my daughter learned quickly that there would be little recourse in modifying their bearing toward the world or shaping them into proscriptive boxes of similar personalities and expressions. They demonstrated their differences from each other in nearly every way possible, from their sleep patterns to the moment they chose to speak their first words, to their temperaments around other people. I still marvel, even decades after having my own children, how swiftly a little child, at first so needy and dependent, begins to open up like a flower into the bloom of its own genuine expression.

I have just entered my seventies, and I look with gratitude over my four children and four grandchildren (and counting). I especially take great joy in watching my grandchildren adopt their own unique ways of being in the world; I'm a bit more seasoned now and am not so surprised by such differences. And yet, I understand the sentiments contained in the countless letters I receive from mothers who are learning this truth for the first time and grappling with its consequences. "How can I get my child to change? I want my child to conform, and I try so hard to train character into them, but no matter what I do, I can't seem to motivate them." Underneath such statements is a singular motivation: "How can I get my children to behave the way I want them to? How can I bring them under my *control*?"

This initial desire is entirely understandable because what we all want as parents is *order* in the midst of the chaos, a sense of predictability. Let me tell you though: holding on to that expectation will only bring you frustration.

You see, you can no more change a child's personality than you can your own. Each child, and indeed every single person alive, is created with their own impossibly complex web of personality traits and opinions and ways of seeing their environment, and this complexity reflects the dynamic artistry of the great master artist who created us all. Even as flowers have infinite colors, shapes, and scents, we too are created with effectively limitless possibilities of potential expression. God delights in this dynamic contrast, and it is part of our faith that we learn to see with God's eyes the glory of His varied creation.

Naturally, this extreme diversity of details might bring your children into conflict with each other, or with you. While such points of tension are all but impossible to avoid altogether, it is entirely possible to cultivate an environment of understanding in which each person is given the chance of being received on their own terms, according to their context. Every personality has a different motivation, and learning these motivations is a key factor to unlocking how different personalities might be woven together in harmony. Slowly, we moved our clan into a unified community with love, respect for each one, and grace for all at the center of our lives.

As Nathan explains, as parents, Clay and I became early proponents of studying the one-of-a-kind design of each of our children, so that from that depth of understanding, we could cultivate an environment of love and acceptance as a family. This didn't mean we eschewed training; to the contrary, we developed a framework of values as a family to which we held each child in turn. To understand particularities isn't to give up on universals; however, when it comes to your children, knowledge is power. And when a child feels understood in their own particular personality, it frees them to trust you, and to become a better listener when you seek to cultivate a space of order and harmony.

From the beginning, we sought to reach our children's hearts, not modify their behavior; we attempted to train from a space of understanding, not a space of conformity. In establishing this foundation of acceptance and affirmation, it made it possible for us to call each of our children into the fuller vision of the values we wished to instill in them, because they trusted that we saw them as they were and would be faithful stewards of their hopes, fears, strengths, weaknesses, and desires.

As I look at my four grown children today, I see in each of them the same personality quirks they had decades ago when they were young children. Each of them has matured in such rewarding ways, and I take great pleasure in seeing the fascinating and full-bodied people they have become; and yet, I also marvel that, in many senses, they are the same people they have always been, even from the very start.

Though I don't know what the whole scope of the story of my grandchildren will be, I have no doubt that they too will only become more of themselves, expressing the beauty of their unique design given them by God. My family is a budding garden of different colors, hues, and expressions, and as I grow older, I see how much God has blessed me in that diversity. I pray that you too will be able to begin the hard work of uncovering the glories hidden in each of your children's hearts, so that you can share in the blessing they have to offer in their own particular ways.

From Nathan:

The whole family—two parents, four kids, and our golden retriever, Kelsey—sat around the dining room table one bright summer day. For the past hour we had been filling out a questionnaire, pens in hand, thinking intently on which answer to choose, which box we'd fill in. And now, we sat waiting with bated breath, my dad holding the results in his hand. The test we took wasn't like many: there were no right or wrong answers, there was no failing. Found within its questions was only discovery—self-discovery. The test was the Myers-Briggs personality assessment, formulated in the mid-twentieth century to help people better understand and quantify human behavior and personality in a way that wasn't restrictive but instead informative.

My dad, interested during his younger years in personality psychology, had become an officially certified MBTI (Myers-Briggs Type Indicator) tester; and now he was putting his training to work to help his family understand themselves and their fellow family members better. One by one, he read our results, each of us listening intently to the descriptions and insights into who we were; each of us discovering we had different and unique combinations of attributes. Some of us were extroverts, others introverts. Some of us oriented toward schedule and order, and others toward inspiration and freedom. Some were visionary, some detailed, and so on. While we didn't know it at the time, what started as a fun family afternoon activity filled with laughter, jokes, and head-nodding became a central theme in our family's interaction and the conduit to greater closeness and celebration of each member's unique, God-created personality.

In the following years, as a result of this initial testing, we each began finding a greater love, appreciation, acceptance, and even celebration of each other and our differences. So often within families, it can be hard to deal with people who live in close proximity to us, who act differently than us. We have thoughts like: "Why can't they just be quieter; why won't they make a schedule; why aren't they more organized; why are their heads always in the clouds; why are they so uptight about cleanliness—why can't they be more like *me*?"

Anyone who has ever had a family knows these everyday struggles. And it's natural for us to assume people acting or living differently than us are acting or living in a wrong way. But for our family, taking the test and exploring its results helped us articulate the beautiful truth of how God created each of our personalities—just like musical notes, colors, and seasons—completely and gloriously unique.

Of course, even now as adults our personalities still clash. I'll be loud when others want to be quiet; someone will make a schedule when others want to feel unconstrained; a parent or sibling will talk about future plans when someone else is focused on today. But even in natural familial conflict, as a result of that family test day, we continue to be pulled back to a core belief: that the differences we encounter in the personality of others aren't bad. They're just different; and this is a good thing.

The test gave us a greater context for each other, and dispelled the notion that when someone acts differently from us, even annoyingly so, it's bad. It instead offered us the freedom to see behavior in others we might've construed as annoying or intentionally wrong as instead part of how they were created to act in the world. And we learned to see that how they act—the personality they bring to the family unit—has inherent value that only they can offer.

As an actor having worked in Hollywood for over a decade, I have learned just how important casting is to the benefit of a play or movie. Every story being told, be it on stage or screen, calls for a diverse set of characters, each with their own unique roles to play within the narrative. The best casts are marked not by how alike they are, but how each member brings something entirely unique to the story, while finding chemistry and connection to other players doing the same. Almost all our favorite movies and TV shows are filled with a brilliantly colorful set of characters who bring something to the story no one else could, not a monolithic set of characters who look and act the same. The same goes for the diverse personalities found in our family—everyone has a unique role to play that is needed and should be celebrated.

While both nature and nurture play a part in the development of a child's personality, decades of studies have led psychologists to discover that at least a large part of a person's personality is completely biological and present from a child's first breath.[1] A large part of what makes up their biology, like their hair or eye color, is there from the beginning. Studies also show that the baseline of a person's personality changes very little over the course of a lifetime, if at all.[2] This means kids are born with much of their personality already intact, and attempts to change their personality into something wholly different is a lost cause. It will only bring about frustration in a parent and pain in the heart of a child who feels they are "bad" for who they were created to be, and equally unable to change.

Of course, unique personalities are a difficult thing to deal with, especially in the context of a large family where imperfect people have to share space, time, and life. But in following God's example of loving and creating all of His children's personalities, we must find the way to celebrate and encourage the personalities He's entrusted to us.

My personality has often been described as "outside-the-box," even aside from my mental illness and learning disabilities. My personality is big: it's open, it asks questions, loves teasing, debates intently, laughs loudly, and explores the unknown with excitement. But often in the outside world, as a result of my personality, I found myself in places where I felt shame for who I was and the personality I had: getting yelled at by teachers, bullied by peers, and ignored by superiors.

This was difficult and brought on doubts about who I was and my own inherent goodness. But when I returned home, those doubts were quickly dispelled within my family who had fostered a belief that my specific personality, no matter how different from my siblings or parents, was a beautiful and ultimately valuable thing. In the walls of my home, both in my childhood and today, is an invitation to be fully myself and celebrate what I specifically bring to the loved ones around me, all while I offer the same outreaching hand to the myriad personalities around me.

Personality tests have had a meteoric rise in popularity in the past fifty years with tests like Myers-Briggs, DiSC, The Big 5, and most recently the Enneagram. This could be a result of many factors, but in the face of modernity where we see increasingly broken families, burnout in the workplace, and the decline of faith—all things that give us insight into who we are and what our personalities are for—people have gone searching for something to give them truth about and validation for who they are. Identity is a core human desire, coded into our minds by God, and personality tests give us perspective into who we are and sometimes even who we were made to be. While none of them can ever fully encapsulate the vastness of the human being, the popularity of these tests shouldn't be ignored as they point to something we are all longing for—the belief that we are unique and the reassurance that this is a good thing.

Any parent of more than one child can testify that regardless of genetics, environment, or conditioning, every child has a completely unique personality. I have testified to my personality being described as outside-the-box, but it's my firm belief that *every* personality, no matter how loud or quiet, abstract or detailed, structured or ordered, is outside-the-box. This is a good thing, one God intended for a reason. And while the world has a vested interest in creating formulaic humans who fit into the prescribed molds, God has given every parent and family the important job of fostering, loving, and reveling in the personalities of its members.

Scripture Reading

Just as a body, though one, has many parts, but all its many parts form one body, so it is with Christ. For we were all baptized by one Spirit so as to form one body—whether Jews or Gentiles, slave or free—and we were all given the one Spirit to drink. Even so the body is not made up of one part but of many.

Now if the foot should say, "Because I am not a hand, I do not belong to the body," it would not for that reason stop being part of the body. And if the ear should say, "Because I am not an eye, I do not belong to the body," it would not for that reason stop being part of the body. If the whole body were an eye, where would the sense of hearing be? If the whole body were an ear, where would the sense of smell be? But in fact, God has placed the parts in the body, every one of them, just as he wanted them to be. If they were all one part, where would the body be? As it is, there are many parts, but one body. (1 Corinthians 12:12–20)

FAMILY DISCUSSION QUESTIONS

1. What do you like about your unique personality?

2. What about your personality is challenging to you that others may not understand?

3. Is it ever hard to get along with people who have a different personality than you?

4. What do you like about your family members' personalities?

5. What are some ways you could grow that might not be natural to your personality?

INTEREST AND SIMPLICITY SHOULD BE THE KEYNOTES OF ALL EDUCATION, I BELIEVE. IT IS IMPOSSIBLE TO FASCINATE YOUNG MINDS WITH DULL COMPLEXITIES.

THOMAS EDISON

CHAPTER THREE

Learning Styles

Dear Sally and Nathan,

We have three children, a son (10), a daughter (8), and a newborn girl. We love each of our children and want the very best for them. But when it comes to school and education, we are at a bit of a loss as to what to do with our son. Our middle daughter is already a high achiever, seemingly finding joy in getting good grades and pleasing teachers. She is well behaved, easily taught, and actually enjoys schoolwork! Our son, on the other hand, is entirely different—he is hyperactive and has an extremely difficult time focusing for long periods of time. Not only does he test poorly, but he also seems to act out in the form of argumentation and is constantly getting in trouble with teachers for talking too much in class. He will only do schoolwork when forced and immediately races outside to bike and build forts with his friends after doing the bare minimum. We want to love him as he is, but we are also very worried about his future and fear his difficulty focusing in school will negatively affect the rest of his life and limit his options of living a healthy and whole life, which every parent wants for their child. We by no means want to force him to be something he's not, but aren't sure how to best love him as he is and still set him up for success.

—Margerie

From Sally:

Early in our marriage, my husband, Clay, and I went on an adventure. After Clay finished his MDiv in Colorado, we took up our first assignment in Vienna, Austria, working on staff with an international chapel there. Vienna sits at the crossroads of western and eastern Europe and has historically acted as a gathering place for people from all over the world. We were no different than many residents of the city, making our own journey from across the Atlantic; and upon our arrival, we were suddenly immersed in a world replete with the crossing currents of different cultures, industries, and languages. Though the services in our chapel were conducted in English, our congregation was made up of people from over forty different countries. Many were diplomats representing their home countries and working at the United Nations in Vienna, and they carried with them the rich traditions of their cultural heritage.

I became especially saturated in this multicultural milieu through the regular dinners and teas I held in our home. Every week brought a different set of guests, and with them, a multiplicity of captivating perspectives and values that I had never encountered before. Every event was a rich education, an immersion in a world of new ideas and viewpoints; and it awakened within me a hunger I didn't know existed, a desire to learn. I realized very quickly that though I had graduated with a good degree from a respectable university and had even learned the basics of four languages, my education was far more limited than I had been able to recognize back home in America. There was so much I didn't know, and the more I was exposed to the broader world beyond the borders of my own knowledge, the more that desire grew.

This experience hit at a crucial point in my life as a wife and mother. I had just become pregnant with my first child, Sarah, and in thinking ahead to being parents, Clay and I decided that we wanted to educate our children differently. At that point, we hadn't heard of home education, but as idealists, we talked endlessly about what aspects we would include in our children's education to cultivate their minds, enrich their vocabularies, widen their areas of knowledge, and empower them to live a life of flourishing and fulfillment. As we benefitted ourselves from the fruitful and soul-expanding conversations happening on a nearly daily basis, we began to formulate a desire that our children would someday be the sorts of people who could have a treasure chest of ideas, wisdom, and knowledge that they could take with them into the world and enrich others.

When our children were old enough, we applied the lessons we learned in Vienna to our home. Over time, we filled our home with books of every kind—history, fine art, classical mythology, natural science, timeless novels—and eventually made a library space where our children could sit and pick any book off the shelf. We brought them to museums to experience great works of visual art firsthand and took them regularly to classical concerts where they could experience the excitement of an orchestral performance. We had days at botanical gardens and nature centers, and often visited historical homes and buildings. We made instruments available to them and encouraged regular playing and singing in our home. In every way possible to us, we made our home a veritable garden of educational delights that invited our children into the wonder of learning.

Of course, this world of home education happened within the contingencies of a hectic family life, involving six people who all wanted to eat three meals a day and wear reasonably clean clothes. It was my ideal that we maintain at least the semblance of an orderly home, a never-ending pursuit always just a hair's breadth beyond my grasp. There were many days amidst the chaos where I doubted my capacities and wondered if my children were learning anything at all.

It was a journey that we took by faith, believing that the holistic approach we were taking would in time reap dividends. While we made sure our children met state educational testing standards, we decided early on not to assign grades, so as to avoid comparison to others or unintentionally make one child or another feel separated by their scores. We used a limited amount of curriculum for subjects that required workbooks like math and language arts; and then the remainder of areas of study we covered through reading aloud, supervised discussions, and assigning reflection essays.

At the heart of our approach was a belief that the best education would come through a mentoring-discipleship approach that highly valued the role of relationship. This was attuned first to our children's relationship with God. We wanted first and foremost to affirm to them that everything they experienced in our home was within the context of a God who loved them and desired for them to know Him. As such, we focused on character development and relating the virtues of the life of Christ as the very foundation of meaningful learning. We wanted them to know that the purpose of education was not to check off some arbitrary list of scholarly achievements, but to become whole people, capable of living into the unique gifts God had given them in their lives.

This meant that we had our own learning curve in adapting to the different educational strengths and weaknesses in each of our children and customizing their learning pathways to their particular needs. One of my children learned to read at an astonishingly early age and consumed books more quickly than I could make them available. Another child had a knack for articulating complex concepts and grasping advanced connections in philosophy and logic but took much longer to learn basic letters and sentences. Despite being uncertain whether they were behind or not, I simply kept a rich stream of new books and engaging discussion active and available to them, and this child didn't miss a beat in their long-term education.

Nathan had great difficulty spelling and understanding correct grammar; and yet, around eleven years old, he came to me with beaming eyes and exclaimed, "I've written a fantasy story, and I want you to read it!" To my utter surprise, he had scribed a lengthy manuscript full of descriptive landscapes, engaging characters, and daring adventures. I was utterly astonished to see an advanced understanding of story-craft arising above incidental spelling mistakes and grammatical errors. Another child, at seven years old, started producing "newspapers" with hand-drawn stories and pictures. Every time I thought I had grasped the limits of each child's ability, they exceeded my expectations and delighted me with their hunger to express themselves.

Looking back, I can see how our approach of giving wide berth to each of our children in their individual educational journeys empowered them to excel and follow bold, unconventional pathways into their own success as adults. Amongst their accomplishments are masters and doctoral degrees from Oxford and St. Andrews; award-winning musical compositions; inspiring, beloved feature-length films; fellowships at preeminent universities; and much more. It isn't a great surprise to either Clay or me that all four are published writers; their own books reflect the rich environment of words, discussions, and reading from our home.

While all these things are heartening to us now, more important than all these things is the knowledge that our children still love us and consider us friends in spite of our many mistakes along the way. They continue to love God and each other, and there is no greater delight I could have as a parent. There are a multitude of approaches to education that can produce excellence of mind and spirit. And yet, we believed—and still believe today—that the best education is one that establishes a foundation of love and respect and sets children free to enter adult life with a strong sense of confidence and grace. This, more than anything, is the message I want to affirm to you in sharing my understanding of education with you. If you can grasp that relational core of learning, first between your children and God, and then between them and you and everyone else whom God brings into their purview, I believe you will see their lives expand and flourish in amazing ways.

From Nathan:

As a teenager, I went a couple times a week to the school down the road with my friends. Because I loved great stories, my parents enrolled me in two classes: English and creative writing. They were next door to each other, and I attended one right after the other. But after a couple months, they seemed hundreds of miles apart. In creative writing, I had a winsome and passionate teacher who loved creativity and sought to bring out the best in his students by sharing his love of words and the stories they could weave. Hanging on the walls were pictures of art and beautiful photographs he hoped would inspire the minds of his students.

In English, I had a strict, no-nonsense teacher who seemed annoyed when I needed help. She focused almost solely on the rules and correct answers on the tests, causing the other students to learn only what they needed to pass, and causing me, the kid with dyslexia and ADHD, to feel completely lost and stupid. At the end of the semester my creative writing teacher gave us an assignment to write a short story, so I quickly got to work coming up with a fantastic world, crafting my description of characters and weaving a short story that I had pulled *ex nihilo* from my mind. It was filled with spelling errors and grammatical mistakes, but upon reading my work, my teacher gave me a soaring grade and high praise, seeing past my human imperfections—those could be worked on—to the creative mind beneath. My English teacher, however, gave us a report and test, and while trying my hardest, she failed me, offering no words of encouragement or guidance.

I am now a bestselling author of eight books and a screenwriter of multiple award-winning movies that have been seen by millions, and I still can't spell "necessarily" without spell check; and I put way, too, many, commas, in, my, sentences. I don't say that to brag; I say that to offer evidence that there are ways to educate a child that acknowledge and nurture the potential that might fall outside the lines we've drawn around intelligence and learning. And inversely, there are ways that are short-sighted and cast the title of "failure" over kids who don't fall into the rigid bounds we've created in our modern educational system that expects, forces, and shoves kids into a mold of standardized testing that has been shown over and over again to not work when predicting future success.

Howard Gardner, an American psychologist and Harvard professor specializing in education, released a book in 1983 called *Frames of Mind*,[1] which explored and detailed his research that led to his well-known and supported theory of multiple intelligences. His hypothesis essentially states there are multiple ways for a child to be intelligent and display intelligence, instead of the very narrow metrics we see so often in modern education, and which we've been conditioned to believe are all-encompassing.

In his theory, there are several unique intelligences,[2] all of which require unique educational methods to cultivate. But in most public schooling environments, only two to three are given attention. This is a dangerous and bad thing. In narrowing our definition of intelligence, which in turn narrows our methods of teaching, we are not only leaving out a great portion of the population of children, but also causing them to believe untrue things about themselves: that they are less-than, dumb, and malfunctioning. Gardner believes that almost every child holds the potential for "genius," but so often that genius never gets recognized because of the blinders we have on when defining intelligence and the discriminatory methods we use in educating kids.

Multiple studies since Gardner's original theory became public have gone on to show how necessary it is to see educational practices as diverse and not attuned only to one monolithic method, as children are each created to learn in different ways. A plethora of research has shown the benefits of looking for and discovering how an individual child will learn the best and finding ways to implement those methods so as to realize a more successful education for the child in question.[3]

Conversely, culture's favorite methodology for assessing the intelligence and educational capacity of a child—standardized testing—has been coming under increased criticism in the past two decades. It is increasingly recognized that its ability to adequately measure the learning ability of a child is limited and doesn't account for a million variables like family life, learning disabilities, mental illness, social status, and personality. In an article published by Infinity Learn, the author has this to say about the efficacy of standardized testing:

> Standardized examinations do not account for the various
> traits unique to each individual, such as home environment
> or mental health. Everyone is different, believe it or not, and

does not have similar advantages or capacity to study and receive extra assistance.[4]

The problem with standardized testing is evident in the name itself, "standard," for no child is standard; each is unique, and this includes their learning style.

———————

I understand this can be overwhelming, especially for parents of multiple kids who each have distinctive education styles and needs. But finding and implementing special educational practices can actually be freeing. There's been so much pressure and comparison when it comes to education, with both parents and children being made to feel inadequate when the traditional educational methods don't work. But when we allow ourselves to step outside of the constraining boundaries of what most of mainstream educational structures pressures us and our kids into, we discover a whole new and brilliant world of learning, allowing the parent to stop feeling like a failure when their child struggles with math tests and helping the kid to feel smart even when they don't get a perfect grade.

There's so much joy in exploring all the beautiful and infinite ways there are to educate a mind and heart. Instead of feeling locked into boring tests, you can read aloud from the greatest literature of all time; instead of memorizing endless monotonous facts, you can conduct your very own experiments in your backyard; instead of scoring your kids on a grid, you can spark discussion at the dinner table and talk for hours about all the big and beautiful subjects there are to wander through.

This intentionally personalized way of education doesn't only make space for each and every learning style; it also creates a more holistic learning experience. It doesn't only live in the pages of a textbook or the walls of a classroom; it creates a possibility of education everywhere, doing everything. This educational philosophy will create a love, rather than dread, for learning in the hearts of your kids. Instead of putting them in a box they were never meant to fit in and that will ultimately make them feel inadequate, it will empower them to live a life of passionate learning in which they discover the world according to the way they were created.

Thomas Edison, one of the twentieth century's greatest inventors, was called "addled"[5] by one of his childhood teachers. They were essentially saying he was dumb as his mind often wandered during schooling hours, and this made it hard to keep up with the other students. His mother ignored the uninformed opinion of the teacher, knowing the potential for greatness she saw in her son. She educated him herself, in a way that was tailored to how he was created to learn; lo and behold, this "addled, dumb" kid grew up to be one of the greatest minds in history. And Thomas Edison's story isn't unique. There are endless tales of children who went on to be great thinkers, inventors, artists, politicians, pastors, doctors, scientists, and leaders, after they almost had their lives and minds discarded because they didn't fit the expected mold.

It was quickly apparent from a young age that I had learning disabilities. I couldn't sit still for long periods of time like my siblings and classmates could; I had trouble reading as the words got mixed up in my head; and I had a tendency to argue and ask too many questions. While often teachers would dismiss me as dumb, troubled, or bad because I didn't learn like the other kids, my parents celebrated me for being insightful, tenacious, and curious.

For my growing-up years, in the context of my family, I only ever experienced the feeling that I was capable, intelligent, empowered, and able. Even when I learned differently than my siblings, it was affirmed as a good thing and just the way I was created to learn. But in formal classrooms, I began to wonder if I was actually dumb. I would stare at the other kids easily understanding the lessons that I was struggling to keep up with, and it birthed in me a lifelong struggle to believe I wasn't defective.

Like my creative writing teacher, my mother saw past my educational struggles to the vast potential she identified, cultivated, and supported. Homeschooling me gave her a chance to tailor her teaching to my unique educational needs. Never once, even with the presence of all my learning disabilities, did she ever believe I was dumb, less capable, or lacking in ability. Instead, being an observant and intuitive parent, she studied me and discovered the way I was *created* to learn—uniquely offering me a life past the designation of "F" so many kids carry with them, a life filled with a love of learning—in the way *I* was made to learn. I carry that with me to this day.

And it turns out that as unique as my learning needs were, so were those of my siblings, each needing an education that didn't try to shove them into a formulaic box but instead gave them specific instruction in the way they were designed to learn. Some of us were kinesthetic and needed to touch, feel, and interact with things to learn; some of us were cerebral and needed time to ponder abstract questions; some of us were literary and loved words; some of us were mathematical and excelled with numbers. But whatever our particular learning styles, in our home, they were celebrated and cultivated.

Scripture Reading

Wisdom, like an inheritance, is a good thing
and benefits those who see the sun.
Wisdom is a shelter
as money is a shelter,
but the advantage of knowledge is this:
Wisdom preserves those who have it. (Ecclesiastes 7:11–12)

FAMILY DISCUSSION QUESTIONS

1. What do you love about learning?

2. What is the hardest part about learning?

3. What is your favorite way to learn?

4. Why do you think educating yourself is important?

5. How are you going to choose to educate yourself every day?

"SO MANY OF OUR DREAMS AT FIRST SEEM IMPOSSIBLE, THEN THEY SEEM IMPROBABLE, AND THEN, WHEN WE SUMMON THE WILL, THEY SOON BECOME INEVITABLE."

CHRISTOPHER REEVE

CHAPTER FOUR

Big Unique Dreams

Dear Sally and Nathan,

My husband and I are the parents to two amazing daughters. They are fifteen and seventeen years old, which, as you know, is the age they have begun looking at their own lives and what they want to do with them when they leave home. My husband and I run a small family business in our hometown where we've lived our entire lives. We've always encouraged the girls to do the things they love and explore their talents and giftings. But we have also, more or less, expected them to end up working at the family business after college, where there'd be guaranteed support and security—not only monetarily but in being near family. So needless to say, we were a bit surprised to begin hearing our daughters' thoughts on what they wanted to do after leaving our home. Our eldest daughter, who loves all things literature, expressed a desire to apply to a college in the UK to study literature with an aim to teach and write. Our younger daughter expressed that she didn't want to go to college at all and instead wants to move to New York City to pursue a career as a dancer. While we are so proud of the talented women they are growing up to be and we do want them to follow God's will for their lives, we are at the same time concerned that these dreams might not be the best paths, especially when it comes to the stability and familial support that a future we can offer them would provide. How do we know how to guide them? How do we know what God's will is for them versus our will for them?

—Anne

From Sally:

From my youth, I dreamed of living a life that mattered. I've always longed to do something worthwhile with the time I've been given, especially to help other people. There has always been a spark in my heart that burns with excitement for discovering the potential hidden in all of life. At times, I dreamed alternately of being a writer, a speaker, a missionary, a professor, and even a diplomat. That unquenchable passion propelled me through many years, always prompting me to ask anew what possibilities might lie within my reach for living well and loving others.

Because of that hunger for a well-lived existence, I quickly developed a devotion to biographies, especially to tales of heroism and bravery. As each story touched a deep place in my heart, I would wonder what God had created me to do and what the scope of my own life would be.

When, in 1977, I was challenged at a student missions conference to consider an opportunity to travel behind the Iron Curtain and join an underground movement to train students in how they could know and serve the God who made them and loved them, I knew my moment had arrived. In the power of the Holy Spirit, I began to imagine how I might invest my gifts to help others encounter the living God and give their hearts to Him. For a year, I traveled and taught in five countries and finally ended up living in Communist Europe. That year was the beginning of a soul satisfaction of desires I had experienced throughout my young life; I knew that it was finally my turn to write my own story.

As joyful as that time was for me, my parents had never really caught the vision for the kind of life I longed to live. They had more practical expectations for me. No matter how many times I explained it to them or tried to help them see, they simply couldn't understand and believed me to be pursuing wild flights of fancy. Long after my missionary years, when I became a successful author, I hoped that they would finally understand my love for teaching and helping people, as if all the frustrating moments of feeling misunderstood and judged would finally be vindicated.

Instead, I was dismayed to discover that they and other members of my extended family were embarrassed of the choices I had made. Somehow, after all the long years of toil and effort to invest my life in a worthwhile way, I was still the black sheep of the family, never quite fitting in or meeting expectations. For years, I kept thinking that if I could just make them understand, they would have an "aha" moment—finally, they would affirm me and perhaps even provide emotional and spiritual support for the hard work of ministry I eventually pursued alongside my husband, Clay. Instead, God gave me an "aha" moment: those family members had already closed their minds to the possibility of seeing me positively, and nothing I could do might change their view of me.

My story is far from uncommon. I know from countless conversations with people from all over the world that many of us struggle with feelings of rejection and have become accustomed to harsh criticism for our choices. That criticism especially hurts when it comes from our parents or family. This is partly because our mothers and fathers are the first and most important relationships in our early lives, and no matter how old we get, that relationship never loses its potency. In a way, we remain children even if we eventually become parents ourselves. And yet, there's another reason our relationships with our parents have such influence over our sense of self: our parents are our first mentors and advisers to recognize our dreams and either stifle them or help them grow.

Early in my faith walk, I began to believe that everyone is given a personality, a set of circumstances, and a smattering of talents through which God might bring light to the world. No life is exactly the same, and people can be called to a wide variety of ways of living. Many throughout Christian history were called to ordinary circumstances and influenced their worlds by daily faithfulness, serving others in love, and remaining attentive to their daily tasks.

An exemplar of this sort of life is Brother Lawrence, a seventeenth-century monk whose many letters were collected posthumously into a classic devotional work titled *The Practice of the Presence of God*. His book focused on the belief that what was done in love for God was what fulfilled a believer's life. He suggested that it is not power or influence or riches that gives our lives definition, but rather living by faith and exercising our dedication to Christ in every task. Brother Lawrence's account is a testament to the fact that even quiet stories, if faithfully lived out, might influence people for generations.

Other stories will involve being thrust into big arenas and opened up to substantial stewardships. Wolfgang Amadeus Mozart and Felix Mendelssohn were recognized in their own times as musical geniuses from childhood and never knew a time when they were not in the public eye. From a young age, Billy Graham appeared before crowds of thousands, preaching the Word fearlessly and witnessing to the gospel. Even Jesus' disciples lived out this sort of calling, being pulled out of simple lives as fishermen and tax collectors into the whirlwind of highly visible ministry. For these figures, their stewardship was to bear that more prominent role with the same grace, faithfulness, and patience as might be required in a quieter life. And yet God created them so that their particular gifts intersected with their vocations.

I believe each of our stories has its own unique set of limits and possibilities and that we are all born with the capacity and agency to live out God's calling through our particular set of circumstances. One of the greatest roles we can play as parents is to help ignite the fire in our children's lives to fulfill the unique persona they have been created to embody, even if their life is different than the one we imagined.

This was a hard-won lesson for me, given that my own family didn't seem to support me in the unique calling God had upon my life; and because of that, I was more able to take its wisdom to heart. Throughout my parenting, I sought to unearth the hopes, desires, and dreams of my own children as they developed through the years.

All human beings have a "designer" quality to them. As an artist, God created such a variety of animals (penguins to kangaroos), trees (willow to pines), and flowers (roses to wildflowers). And so it is with humans and their unique DNA, fingerprints, personalities, and physical attributes. It is clear that God values diversity in His creation. And so must we. Rather than judging each person's individual attributes according to our own standards of what is good and acceptable, how important it is that we look at the heart of who a person was created to be. Accepting differences and learning to understand heart motivations for antics, behavior, or actions is of profound importance to validating a person's worth, or indeed all people's worth, as a masterpiece crafted by God. To respect each person's uniqueness is to worship God for His wonderful design.

In practical terms, this process required my willingness to listen and observe my children, letting their giftings and unique drives present themselves to me over time.

Sarah showed an unusual proclivity for words, reading and writing and gobbling up thousands of books in a short period of time. At eleven years old, she developed a desire to attend Oxford, where so many of her favorite authors had also studied. It seemed impossible to me at the time, but I prayed with this child that if it was the right direction for her, God would open up the pathway. God indeed made a way for her. In time she received both her undergraduate and master's degrees from Oxford, while writing numerous books. And now she lives there with her husband and four children.

Joel started singing perfectly on pitch at eighteen months old, and his prodigiousness with music only grew with time. We did what we could to support him along the way, providing instruments and lessons as we could manage. God did the rest and took him to a prominent music college, where he received a degree in composition and has now seen his music performed all over the world.

As a little boy, Nathan was acting out stories with our big box of costumes and play swords. Believing that stories were inspiring to all people to give them a vision for possibilities to a life well-lived and intentional, I could never have imagined that my own child would actually be able to make a living as an actor and movie producer, and yet we opened up opportunities for him along the way in dramatic arts and acting. Today, he is a successful screenwriter, producer, and actor, making inspirational films that are shown to thousands.

From her teen years, Joy was determined to be an academic. She set her mind to that path, and though neither Clay nor I are in the academic world, we attempted to open up opportunities for her to engage in critical thinking, writing, debating, and speaking. She would go on to earn her PhD at twenty-six and is now a research fellow at a prominent university in England.

All my children had individual dreams, tailored to their own personalities and desires. All of them have learned that moving toward ideals takes determination, endless hard work, buckets of faith, and a good dose of steadfastness. Yet, all four have found great satisfaction in being free to follow the dreams their talents and capacities opened within them as children.

All lives tell a different story, and all of us are uniquely created by God to live our lives according to the hopes and desires and work He has set within us. An essential part of our role as parents is simply not to suppress these variances amongst our children. Studies have shown that while children have an unencumbered sense of imagination at a young age, they begin to be heavily influenced by peer pressure during school years.[1] Their desires shift from a hunger to experience the world, to wanting to conform and please their parents, friends, and other authorities.

Some of this is simply natural childhood development. But, as parents, we have a choice in these pivotal years: either to squelch what curiosities and desires remain present through those changing times, so as to make it easier for us to manage them; or to help them embrace their own unique gifts and hopes. Then, when they become young adults, they're already empowered in their particular vocations to be ready to enter the arena fearlessly and with a sense of purpose and direction.

As I look back on my life, I see how writing my many books, teaching countless people, and speaking all over the world has filled my soul with joy and has been deeply heart-satisfying. By God's grace, and despite setbacks along the way, I was able to follow a stewardship I was made to fulfill. And I pray that all children will have the freedom to be validated for the work that God has uniquely put on their hearts. Then, as parents, we will dream with them toward the respective futures they long to pursue.

I have come to terms with the fact that my parents did not understand my choices, which were so different from the ones they made and would have made for me. I have put to rest some of the conflict my family and I experienced because of my outside-the-box choices. Through this journey, I have deepened my sympathy and compassion for others who have experienced negative input and criticism from their own families for living outside the expectations that have been passed down.

From Nathan:

I excitedly searched through the website on the computer screen. It was a site for an acting school in New York City. I scrolled through pictures of groups of friends filming movies in a big city and performing on stages, and acting coaches guiding their students in studios. Every picture excited me as I felt this was an answer to a question I had been asking.

I was eighteen and looking at the rest of my life, trying to figure out what exactly I should do. All my friends had gone off to college, and I was left alone in a small town wondering what the next step was. I had always had big dreams, passions, and loves, but finding how those desires fit into a life plan had my parents and me a bit stumped. I had thought about applying to a nearby state school, but my previous experiences with tests, schoolwork, and class environments had taught me that I didn't exactly thrive in those contexts.

When I made the decision not to attend that university and talked it through with my parents, they agreed, despite pressure from their friends to make me go. But my parents knew me—who I was and what God had placed on my heart to do—and they could see, through faith, that doing the thing everyone said I "should" do wasn't necessarily the thing that was best for me. It felt good making a decision to *not* do something that was right for me, but it left my parents and me wondering what the *right* decision was.

I had always wanted to be an actor, writer, and filmmaker. Since I was young, my passions oriented me to performances, storytelling, and playing pretend. But unlike many professions, my dreams didn't have a formula I could follow for success. Even so, my parents were dedicated champions of each of their kids' desires, and so in an effort to help me discover a way forward that was in line with my passions and dreams, my mom signed me up for an acting conference in Orlando, Florida. It was expensive—very expensive—between flights, hotel, and registration. It definitely made a dent in the wallets of an already hardworking family with multiple kids and endless expenses. But it was a decision my parents felt necessary to make. They saw this as an investment in my future; and supporting my dreams and helping me find a way forward was the reason they had worked as hard as they had.

As a result of their choice, I was able to meet, connect, and commune with other actors, and an acting coach from New York City, who, after seeing me perform, offered me a small scholarship to the New York Film Academy. New York City was the place where I began my adult life and began living out the dreams God had placed on my heart. But it was only possible because my parents had enough trust in God and His unique plan for me and a willingness to support me with their time, money, and counsel to launch me into the life I was made for.

Their support and dedication didn't begin at the end of our childhood. Rather, it was a philosophy that affected how they viewed us and guided us from the very beginning. As my siblings and I grew, our mother and father studied us and considered our natural giftings, desires, skills, and dreams. When I was just a kid, my mom saw that I lit up when she was reading fantastic stories to me or watching great movies, and how I loved acting them out even after the book or movie was over. So, she went to book fairs and bought thousands of great books to line our shelves, and she built a library of VHS adventure movies. She found old costumes in a thrift store with which she filled a chest in my room, so that I could continue living into the dreams that were already forming in my six-year-old heart.

Later, when I was a teen, I became interested in sleight-of-hand and stage magic, so my dad took me to a magic conference in Denver. We made weekly trips to a magic shop where I would spend my allowance on tricks. My parents clapped and cheered wildly when I performed my first show at our church. They couldn't know or see what the outcome of their investment in my childhood interests would be. But all of it helped define and prepare me for living out the dreams that pulled me into my calling.

They trusted by faith that investing in my dreams would help me discover my story. I currently live in Hollywood and New York City, acting in commercials, movies, and TV shows, making my own films for Netflix, and writing bestselling books, all because my parents trusted God enough to support their child's unique, outside-the-box dreams.

They did this for all of their kids. They believed there was a completely unique calling on each of our lives that would shape unique vision—dreams that wouldn't look the way people/culture/friends/teachers/the internet said they should look; dreams that would look different from what *they* might want for us; and dreams that would be unique from the dreams of their other children.

My older sister, Sarah, showed an early love for words and poetry, so they gave her an entire library with classic books, found her a writer's studio, and helped her write, edit, and publish her own book when she was a teenager. Now, she is an Oxford graduate and author of five books.

My older brother showed a talent and drive for music and composition, so they found music teachers to train him, bought a myriad of instruments, and took him to music conferences that would further his knowledge and ability. Now he is a graduate of Berklee College of Music, the composer of more than a dozen popular original instrumental albums, and has had his orchestrations and compositions played in movies, concert halls, and even at the Vatican.

My little sister was a lover of education, debate, and thought. So, my parents enrolled her in speech and debate, hosted an "Inklings" group in their home, and drove her to competitions. Now, she has a doctorate from St. Andrews, has published three books, teaches at King's College London, and is an online and podcasting figure with tens of thousands of followers.

Now, all of us kids are thriving in our completely unique lives, having been given support, guidance, help, and resources to explore and discover what we were made to do and accomplish in the world.

Dreams are an interesting subject in the world, especially in the context of making a living or finding a career. There is naturally a lot of fear around the topic, especially when trying to guide kids into a life where they can support themselves and pay their bills. But in helping kids find who they are and what they're supposed to do, that fear *every* parent will feel should not factor into how they act and guide their kids. My parents decided to not let fear guide their decisions; instead, they lived by faith. But faith in what? Faith in God having designed every human with amazing potential, beautiful purpose, and a unique story to tell.

So often we see, in families and in culture at large, how parents are well-meaning, but ultimately the fear they unintentionally instill causes pain and regret in the children who become adults. It's a regular occurrence displayed in movies and our conversations with friends: people talk about the dreams they wished they'd followed, but because they were pressured to do something they weren't meant to and never given the encouragement, tools, or guidance, they ended up in lives and professions that drain them, make them feel useless, or sometimes don't succeed at all.

Research supports the idea that dreaming big as a child will produce positive results for the whole of life. A long-term study, following 17,000 children via ten surveys from 1958 through 2022, found that the bigness of a child's dreams mattered as much or more than their IQ or socioeconomic status in that child achieving higher success in their desires and passions.[2]

It's natural to want to temper our children's expectations so they aren't crushed by inevitable disappointments. But it turns out encouraging them to dream big will have positive results. This doesn't mean we just blindly encourage every whim a child might have. We've all heard the "follow your dreams" mantra quoted endlessly in movies, written on gift cards, and painted on posters. And while this phrase is usually used with good intentions, we also instinctively know that promising your child they'll be the next NFL quarterback or pop-music sensation will not likely be realized. So, how do we both encourage our children's dreams while at the same time not setting them up for disappointment and failure?

As an actor, I interact daily with fellow aspiring performers who often talk about what they'll say when they win their Oscar. And while this is often good fun, it can be detrimental if taken to an extreme. When I was younger, I would often dream of accepting the great acting award, imagining what I'd say as everyone applauded. But in recent years, what I've been amazed by and what has filled me with joy hasn't been the awards (that I might never win) but the fact that I get to make my living doing what I love. It's not the unrealistic dreams that make me happy but the fact that I pay my bills by getting to do what I was created to do, even if that's acting in a small indie movie or delivering one line on a TV show.

When it comes to figuring out how to balance telling our children to dream big and protecting them from disappointment, the secret is helping them craft a dream without restraint, but one they actually have a path toward and a realistic way of pursuing.

This dream won't look like you expected or what your friends, family, or the experts say it should, but it should be one that coincides with the natural God-given skill set, passions, and proclivities of your child. What this looks like practically isn't so much some unrealistic metric like winning an Oscar, playing for the NFL, or singing to ten thousand fans in Madison Square Garden—those might happen! But if they do, they're just the by-product of helping your child live a life where every day they get to live out their passions and use their skills. The parents' job is to help the child both discover and piece together a worthy and beautiful vision of a dream they can follow for a lifetime. You can encourage your children to dream big, then you can help them discover the dream they were made to dream big about.

My parents saw it as their calling to trust God and believe that He was the one who would make it clear what each of their children were made for and who they were made to be. They did this by asking themselves a few questions as they studied, loved, guided, and helped us find the paths God had for us and realize the dreams He had placed on our hearts.

1. *What do they love?* The first thing my parents would look for when helping us discover our dreams and calling was to identify what we were most passionate about doing, most naturally drawn to over a long period of time, and what made us light up when we did it. This helped them catch a vision for the things in our lives that could give us a lifetime of joy and passion.

2. *What are they good at?* They would then see where our natural ability was, what we excelled at, and where our skills were. Taking this into account, in combination with our loves, helped them find ways to apply our natural skill set to things we could also be emotionally fed by and have a passion for.

3. *What's next?* They would look at our skill sets and passions to then find ways they could help us grow in them and hone them, whether through classes, resources, conferences, groups, tutors, or books. But whatever it was that we showed a skill and passion for, they looked for ways to further our ability and knowledge in it.

It's hard ignoring the voices of culture and people around us, much less our own fears when it comes to guiding children into adulthood and into the realization of their vocations. But by grasping, by faith, that God has created every child with abilities and dreams specific to them and for a unique purpose, we can begin to let go of fear and step into the great and glorious adventure that is believing in and with our children, as they set out to discover the story God has for them to tell. Their story won't look like the story of the kid sitting next to them; it may not look like the one we planned for them; and it won't look like the one culture wants to tell; but it will be wonderful and beautifully theirs.

Scripture Reading

For it is by grace you have been saved, through faith—and this is not from yourselves, it is the gift of God—not by works, so that no one can boast. For we are God's handiwork, created in Christ Jesus to do good works, which God prepared in advance for us to do. (Ephesians 2:8–10)

FAMILY DISCUSSION QUESTIONS

1. What are your biggest dreams?

2. What are you naturally good at doing?

3. What do you love to do?

4. How would you use your dreams to help the world?

5. Do you think your dreams are given to you by God?

OUR MOST BASIC EMOTIONAL NEED IS NOT TO FALL IN LOVE BUT TO BE GENUINELY LOVED BY ANOTHER, TO KNOW A LOVE THAT GROWS OUT OF REASON AND CHOICE, NOT INSTINCT. I NEED TO BE LOVED BY SOMEONE WHO CHOOSES TO LOVE ME, WHO SEES IN ME SOMETHING WORTH LOVING. THAT KIND OF LOVE REQUIRES EFFORT AND DISCIPLINE. IT IS THE CHOICE TO EXPEND ENERGY IN AN EFFORT TO BENEFIT THE OTHER PERSON, KNOWING THAT IF HIS OR HER LIFE IS ENRICHED BY YOUR EFFORT, YOU TOO WILL FIND A SENSE OF SATISFACTION—THE SATISFACTION OF HAVING GENUINELY LOVED ANOTHER.

GARY CHAPMAN

CHAPTER FIVE

Love Languages

Dear Sally and Nathan,

I'm a mom to triplets! While many parents talk about the difficulties of the infant and toddler stages, I actually found those stages to be (in some ways) easier than the new phase of life we are entering. When my children were younger, they all, more or less, needed the same kind of love and attention from me. To be held, fed, exercised, etc. But suddenly, as they've turned four, it seems everything has changed. They each are starting to develop completely unique needs, and what used to work for all of them, now only works for one or none of them. While one of my children will want to be with me all the time, following me from room to room, another will want to be alone and have independent play. When one wants me to hold, kiss, and hug them regularly, another will want me to just sit and talk with them, and the other will simply ask me to help them do things. I want to give my children the love they each desire and need, but often I feel at a loss for how to do that. I'm naturally an affectionate mama, so some "love languages"[1] are easier for me than others, and trying to understand and give each of them what they want, especially as they all differ, is turning out to be a harder task than I had expected.

—Meagan

From Sally:

Pregnancy was never easy for me. I gained fifty pounds with each child, and even though I eventually lost most of it as water weight, I endured swollen ankles, hands, and face for most of each pregnancy. Morning sickness afflicted me all nine months and might visit me morning, noon, or night. Of course, everyone had advice for me as to how to remedy these maladies, but nothing worked.

These moments left me needing more rest and quiet than usual, and it was during just such a moment of ailing and waiting out the long months in expectation that I was visited with an epiphany about my children. I was late term, fully filling up the chair where I was gladly relaxing for just a tiny reprieve, when one of my littles pattered up to me, blanket in hand, and muttered in their toddler voice, "Mama, I want to be *wif* you. Can I sit wif you, and we can be friends?"

Recently, that same child, now a grown adult with a busy life, was home for a holiday visit. The fireplace was lit, Christmas tree lights were sparkling, an assortment of candles emitted the sweet scent of vanilla, and seasonal music wafted gently by in the background. As I sat on my sofa and relished the beauty around me, in walked my thirty-something child. This one sat next to me, and said, "Let's steal a moment here together. How about we sit here a while and just 'be friends'?"

In the never-ceasing, joyful cacophony of our talking, arguing, laughing, feasting family, it has always been a bit of a challenge to carve out space to be totally alone with each of my children. There is often an uncanny coordination of interruptions the moment the silence settles, and cherished conversation ensues. But I learned many years ago that this particular child, an introvert often lost in the exuberant whirlwind of our family, needed time alone to be seen and heard properly. It was very important to them that they be understood, and even a little bit of listening and responding might transform this child's disposition. As a consequence, over many years, whenever I know that child will be home, I make sure to set aside quality time as I know it is a way to their heart, a means of cultivating companionship and remaining dear friends.

The way each of us best receives expressed love is a powerful way to identify what each child's heart values and to meet them in that desire. Though I personally believe that all of us need multiple expressions of love, it is clear that certain kinds of affection and attention speak in different ways to different people. In this way, Jesus has always been my muse and model. He exemplified all of these expressions, from using validation, saying to Peter, "You are the rock!"; to offering the lowliest of service to His disciples, washing 120 man-toes at the Last Supper, and then providing a delicious meal for His weary friends afterward. He generously sacrificed His life for the well-being of all His loved ones, giving them His time, friendship, attention, and instruction so that they would personally understand and know God's love. And He called them into the same life of self-giving, instructing them that "the world will know you are my disciples by your love for one another."

Consequently, there are multiple ways I might seek out my children through different modes of love and affection, I know that I am only following Christ, who enacted the fullness of self-giving before me. I take my cues from Him. Of course, there are more general ways to convey our love to our children, not the least of which is by simply telling them we love them. But those words alone are not enough; if time, attention, and helping are not part of the warp and woof of our lives with our children, those words will ring empty, lacking the integrity they promise to fulfill.

I don't mean to downplay the challenges involved in this process. Trust me when I say I understand because I came to mothering unprepared, untrained, and without an understanding of the differences there would be in my children. I had a long and, at times, arduous learning curve in apprehending the parameters of each of my children. And yet, because I had always longed for unconditional love and affirmation, I approached parenting with a desire to ensure that my children would always sense my unconditional love for each of them.

The word "love" occurs over three hundred times in the Bible; if something is that prevalent in Scripture, it demands my attention. You see, love is the oxygen that fills our hearts with the breath of life, and without love, we feel ourselves straining to go on and stay strong. The love we receive as children profoundly shapes our lives, and for those who don't receive love at a young age, they may end up chasing after that love their whole lives, never knowing they are safe, seen, and adored.

Let me share with you some of the unique ways I've learned to love my children.

From almost the moment he had any words at all, Nathan wanted to talk and talk. He has always been a verbal processor and desired to air each and every thought so that it might be heard and validated. As such, personal time and intentional attention are high on Nathan's list of relationship priorities. He once told me: "Mama, when you spend time with me alone, it makes me want to obey you. When I feel ignored, I'll do whatever I need to do to get your attention." Let me tell you that out of the mouth of our children often comes the truth we need!

I was surprised to find that one of my girls felt particularly loved when I packed her suitcase or washed a load of clothes for her. Even today, it makes her feel seen and taken care of when

I tend to these basic tasks. Serving practical needs is a way into relationship with her.

My other daughter adores receiving cards, letters, photos, and text messages. She longs for love and kindness, and so I've learned that expressions of encouragement are particularly important for her.

Some things, I have learned, are universal and can make all four of my children feel blessed. I have found that a cup of tea, a warm chocolate chip cookie, and ten minutes of time together is nearly always a winner in our family.

I offer these not as an exhaustive list by any stretch of the imagination, but as small windows into my own experience, in the hope that perhaps they can give you ideas of what may work in your life and with your children. Despite all my flaws through the years, I have found that investing in the reality of love that attends to each child's needs has built close and intimate friendships with all four of my children, and sparked the sort of love in me that satisfies deep places in my own soul.

Love acted out is the adhesive that holds the whole of your family together. When you express abundant love in time, service, affection, affirmation, and attention, you will see your child grow in confidence and peace, gaining a deeper sense of belonging in their world. Without that love, it won't matter how many experiences, opportunities, or material possessions you may provide for your children; they simply can't thrive unless everything is constructed upon a foundation of love. And constructing a strong foundation of expressed love requires work on your part to research the ground on which you are building that strong tower, to understand the special nature of each child in whom you are investing your time and attention. By investing in love, intimacy, and friendship in a way that made sense to each of my children, I helped them know that they belonged to our little community called "Clarkson." They could always know that in this place, they would be held, loved, and seen.

As I was writing this chapter, Nathan came by my office door to see me. "Hey, let's make sure to have several times just for you and me to talk about everything in the world. You know I always want to be with my mama!" From my own experience, I can tell you that the shelter of love you are building through your relationships with your children now will last a lifetime.

As we become more seasoned parents, we understand more fully the need for friendship and love amongst our children, and we gain a deeper appreciation for how to invest in a way that attends to each of their particular needs. In developing an awareness of these factors, we are doing more than going through the motions; we are opening up the possibility of deep and abiding relationships. This is the example Jesus sets for us in His friendships: not only words said, but His whole life given as a sacrifice of praise, to express His love for those in His care in tangible ways. In Jesus, we have a pattern to follow: in giving up our lives as a sacrifice of praise and as a service of love, our children will be liberated to know that God is a loving God, mirrored in our actions.

From Nathan:

I remember so viscerally one of those difficult teenage days. The kind of days that feel utterly overwhelming for an adolescent struggling with insecurity, anxiety, mental illness, and the pangs of growing up. I walked through the door to our house after a tiring day of classes, letting my backpack thud to the floor before I made a straight path to the shelter of my bedroom. Many days can be hard as a teenager, but this one in particular had taken an especially large chunk from my young heart.

The day had been layered in insecurity-inducing pain, beginning with my crush rejecting me for another guy after I had gathered up the courage to tell her I liked her. Her rejection caused me to compare myself to him and find all the ways in which I was lacking. After enduring the pain of young romantic rejection, I had then found myself the subject of bullying by the popular group of teens, calling me things so cruel I can't even write them down. To finish off the day, a teacher had given me back an assignment covered in red marks and a less than satisfactory grade. All of this happening in the course of a few hours had underlined my fear that I was unattractive, uncool, and dumb.

I look back now and just want to hug my younger self and tell him to keep his head up. But in the midst of the chaos of teenage angst almost nothing could compete with the harsh, careless, and painful words I had been subject to that day. In my room, I fell onto my bed with a deep and meaningful sigh. I looked around my room; in the few hours I had been absent from it, it had been cleaned by my mom and had a fresh basket of laundry by my chest of drawers. On the shelves stood my recent collection of action figures and books, and on the walls were new posters, all of which my parents had given me for Christmas. The gifts surrounding me, and the ways my family served me should've reminded me how much I was loved and cherished, but the salve that my heart longed for wasn't found in their presence.

I heard a gentle knock at my door.

"Come in," I said in a less than enthusiastic voice.

My mom entered, having seen me return home with my head hung low. Entering with a paper plate full of warm chocolate chip cookies, she smiled and said, "I just want to spend time with my wonderful Nathan." She asked me how I was, how my day went, and what was going on.

I was coy at first, not wanting to spill too many of my deep emotions out lest I feel completely pathetic on top of everything. But with gentle, motherly prodding, my mom coaxed out the truth about the humiliation, self-hatred, and insecurity I was feeling. She created a safe place for me to pour out my heart in my time and my way, and when I was done, she looked me in the eye and said, "Nathan, I know you must feel so down right now, and I know you are experiencing a lot of self-doubt. But I want you to know, you are special, you are deeply intelligent, you are handsome, and you are destined for great and amazing things."

As she spoke those words, they spread over me like a salve, her words of life drawing out the sting from the words of pain that had been said to me by others and myself. Because of her dedication to understand the person God had designed me to be, my mother knew how to love me and how I was made to receive love. She knew that words held the power of life to me, so when I was torn apart, she knew that it would be through the language of love that her son would be put together again.

───────────

In his wildly popular book *The 5 Love Languages,* Gary Chapman identifies the five main ways humans give and receive love. The love languages are: Receiving Gifts, Quality Time, Words of Affirmation, Physical Touch, and Acts of Service. The book suggests that each of us, while appreciating and even needing all of the love languages, are specifically made to respond most strongly to just one or two. For millions of people and relationships, this has provided an extremely helpful grid for understanding human emotional needs. The concept of love languages points to something in our very design: the first being that all of us were made to receive love; and the second being that all of us are made to receive love in unique ways, which is a wonderful thing!

Similar to learning any language, learning someone's love language can also be a difficult task that will require insight and practice. While we all receive love in different ways, we likewise have our preferred ways of giving love. And sometimes the love that a child or loved one needs from us falls outside the lines of our preferred way to offer it, which is why it's such an important task to grasp this concept of how uniquely each of us was created to receive love. Perhaps you feel more comfortable washing someone's dishes or doing their laundry, when what they really needed to feel loved was a back scratch. Or maybe you pride yourself on your gift giving ability when what your child really wants is to be told you're proud of them for getting an A+.

A study conducted on the Love Languages theory found that, in romantic relationships, simply knowing your partner's love language could predict a greater relationship satisfaction both in the present and the future.[2] The same is true for a relationship between a parent and child. When a parent takes the time to understand their child's unique need for love and their unique way of expressing it, they are understanding an intrinsic part of that child's soul; and when it's understood, it can be fed, then it will be fed, and from that point it can grow. Learning how each of our family members both show and receive love has a lifegiving effect on everyone. Speaking a child's love language enables them to move about the world with more freedom and support, as if they are riding on a steady stream of love, understanding, and support as they walk confidently through life.

The birthday tradition in the Clarkson family goes like this: after the presents have been opened, the feast has been eaten, and the whole family sits around the table, one by one, we offer the birthday boy or girl a few words about how we've seen them grow that year, what we hope for the next year, and what we love about them most. It's a sacred and beautiful moment when, once a year, that person can be still and have words of love surround and encourage them, spoken by the ones they hold most dear. Of course, I loved the presents and the cinnamon rolls; but as I look back into my childhood, these moments during which my family surrounded and loved me with their words stand out as having had a far-reaching and positive effect on my life. This is because I was made to be loved with words.

Every child will need a specific and tailored love, and it's the job of a parent to identify and give this love in the way God has created them to receive it. I love that Gary Chapman uses the word "language" when speaking about love because learning to love someone is very much the same as learning a language. It's a process of education and understanding that guides us in the art of communication. When we don't know how to speak someone's language, we can feel we are at a loss at how to communicate vital information. So, to love every child well, we must learn the language of love God has created for them to receive. And more often than not, it won't be your preferred way to offer love. But in the same way that God offers us a unique love, tailored to our needs, He asks parents to do the same.

Scripture Reading

Be sincere in your love for others. Hate everything that is evil and hold tight to everything that is good. Love each other as brothers and sisters and honor others more than you do yourself. Never give up. Eagerly follow the Holy Spirit and serve the Lord. Let your hope make you glad. Be patient in time of trouble and never stop praying. Take care of God's needy people and welcome strangers into your home.

Ask God to bless everyone who mistreats you. Ask him to bless them and not to curse them. When others are happy, be happy with them, and when they are sad, be sad. Be friendly with everyone. Don't be proud and feel that you know more than others. Make friends with ordinary people. Don't mistreat someone who has mistreated you. But try to earn the respect of others, and do your best to live at peace with everyone. (Romans 12:9–18 CEV)

FAMILY DISCUSSION QUESTIONS

1. What is your favorite way to be shown love?

2. What is your favorite way to show love to others?

3. What is the hardest way for you to show love to others?

4. How can you love people around you better?

5. Why do we all need to give and receive love?

RATHER THAN TRUSTING GOD, MANY WILL DOGGEDLY HOLD ONTO THE BELIEF THAT THERE IS A DIVINELY-DESIGNED FORMULA OR BIBLICAL METHODOLOGY THAT CAN ENSURE THEIR CHILD'S SALVATION, AND THEN GUARANTEE THE CHILD'S SANCTIFICATION. THAT DEBATABLE BELIEF OFTEN LEADS TO **FINDING SPECIAL METHODS IN SCRIPTURE** THAT COME WITH A PROMISE OF SUCCESS. SOON, THOUGH, THE PARENTS ARE NO LONGER TRUSTING GOD, BECAUSE THEY NO LONGER NEED TO—**THEY ARE TRUSTING THE METHODS INSTEAD.** THOSE METHODS, THEN, CAN TOO EASILY BECOME RULES, AND THEN LEGALISM, AND THEN **A RELIANCE ON WORKS THAT REPLACES A LIFE OF FAITH.**

CLAY CLARKSON

CHAPTER SIX

Heartfelt Discipline

Dear Sally and Nathan,

My husband and I are the mom and dad of three very different boys aged nine, ten, and thirteen. I grew up in a house full of girls, which did nothing to prepare me for raising three rambunctious boys. My husband is very involved and helps draw boundaries for the boys' energy. But as we homeschool and my husband works during the day, much of the discipline during waking hours lies in my hands. In my house growing up, having a good cry and talk seemed to do the trick, but that doesn't seem to be the way my boys respond when it comes to discipline, and I end up being ignored or run over. Some people have suggested we spank them to get better results. But my husband and I just don't feel comfortable with that. That leaves us unsure of how to reach and teach them. We want to be both loving and engaged, but often it feels as if our attempts are in vain. We would love some insight on how to move forward.

—Kathryn

From Sally:

When the doctors placed Sarah, my first baby, into my arms, I was overcome with wide-eyed wonder. It had been a long and arduous labor, and her little red face showed the signs of the use of forceps. And yet, as she nestled against my chest and I felt her steady breath, her dark blue eyes cast a spell of "forever love" over me.

Things were difficult for Sarah at first; she had to stay in the ICU for three days and experienced health problems that, to me as a first-time mother, were frightening. After she was finally well enough to come home, she was almost never out of my arms or sight for the first couple of years. I nurtured her and cherished her presence, loving her with all my heart and desiring to help her grow and thrive.

As a mother of four children, I have come to see just how profoundly important those first few years of life are to the training and discipline of children. Before they were old enough to fully understand their own volition or agency, before they could assent to being obedient or follow my directions, I was already holding my babies, attending to their needs and desires, and talking to them incessantly. That dedicated attention already started forming them in ways that would affect their whole lives and would set a foundation of love for all that would come after.

So often, we as parents long for a prescriptive approach to discipline. We wish there were an instruction book with clear directions on what paths to take and what methods to implement. However, no child responds to correction in exactly the same way, and discipline applied too generally often counteracts positive growth.

I saw this often in my own life. Two of my children were self-governing, sensitive to my input and expectations. They were rule keepers by nature; I could almost just look at these children and they would melt. They were both introverts and had a strong inner sense of their place in the world.

My other two pushed back at me a bit more, defending themselves and their behavior. They were more extroverted and opinionated, more assured of their own rightness. And they also had soft hearts, and with patience and time, I could count on them to apologize or make peace with Clay and me.

Many parents have come to believe that discipline is an issue of controlling a child's behavior. For us, child discipline was about shaping our children's hearts, helping them develop their own sense of virtue, so that they could grow in time into complete and flourishing adults. Our goal was to give them a vision for living a life pleasing to God, based on His own love and grace for us.

Performative child training often looks for a child to replicate a given command and judges them based on their ability to maintain that behavior—which, of course, they won't be able to do perfectly. In each instance they fail to meet that established standard, performative child training produces an internal sense of guilt, a feeling that "I'll never be good enough to please Mom and Dad." Guilt is a poison that destroys the heart and belief that God is good and loving, and a child may carry it with them for a lifetime.

By contrast, relational training sees the child as a fully fledged human being in their own right, needing assistance to move from immaturity toward maturity. Relational parenting avoids totalizing a child's behavior in the moment, but rather sees it within that longer stretch between childhood and adulthood, as part of an ever-expanding process over which we as parents are stewards.

Let me share with you some ways I sought to shape my own children's hearts through unconditional love:

I gave them **words of life** even before they fully understood what I was saying. As I held one of my littles in a sling, I said to them, "Look at that beautiful sunset that God created. I wonder if pink and coral and gold are some of His favorite colors. How God must love us to give us such a gift."

I sang lullabies to them each night and often rocked them to sleep, **praying over them and blessing them.** Cultivating that attachment through love, gentleness, and affection prepares them to be more receptive to us as parents.

When an offense was committed, I made sure to **fully attend to the offense and not gloss over it.** I would often take my littles into my arms and leave the room, going somewhere quiet where we could talk. I would make sure they understood why I was taking them aside and ask, "Do you know why I asked you to come with me out of the room?" Dialogue was always essential, because as a parent, I am not merely correcting my child; I am a human speaking to another human in relationship, helping them own their decisions and make better ones.

Once that discussion had been opened up, I would then **provide correction and counsel, avoiding harshness**, saying, "We only use our hands for gentleness, never to hit someone." Or: "Mama wants you to obey me when I call you because I love you and am here to protect you." Through that relational approach, I made sure my children felt understood and heard, and in that way were able to properly receive the correction I had to offer. And yet, we did ask for growing obedience and respect according to their ages and understanding.

I **focused highly on self-control** and on each child owning their own behaviors. I would use language that would empower them to make their own decisions, rather than me simply telling them what to do. For example: "I know you are frustrated, but Mama is allergic to whining. When you can talk to me in a normal voice, I'll be able to help you with what you need." We gently encouraged our children to understand that they had agency to be able to respond to us and learn to grow in obedience as we talked, held, and trained throughout their younger years.

By practicing being attentive, we were more able to make the training appropriate to their age and needs. In other words, if they were exhausted by staying up too long, they needed sleep, not correction. If their behavior was out of character with their personality, we searched for understanding what their behavior was reflecting. If we had not had enough personal time with our children, sometimes they would act out their needs to secure our attention.

We felt the pathway to learning how to grow "strong" inside was based on teaching them to understand that they had the ability to rule over their emotions, to make choices to be kind to siblings, to honor us by learning to obey. Growing in self-control was a process of learning wisdom and of understanding the value of relationships, over times of repetition. We used our words not to control our children, but to help them to know they had the ability to make wise choices that would end up blessing them.

We worked hard to **not ignore our children when they expressed a need**—even when they were complaining. Often, whining, complaining, and crying are the only ways a young child knows to get the attention of a parent who habitually doesn't pay attention to them. In this way, relational child training requires us to change our behavior as parents as well and to be attentive in order for them to feel heard and understood, which often led to their ceasing with having to whine to get our attention.

These are, of course, very limited examples of what we enacted in our home. But we were training, training, training every day, all the time.

In sharing these examples, I want to stress that these are not rules to follow, but principles that worked for us and might be helpful for you. They are not prescriptive, and every child needs something a little different. Relational child training is always a matter of adapting according to your children in what they need at the time. It is a more invested approach, but it also reaps more rewards in the long run.

And discipline isn't only a matter of negative behavior; it is equally a regular affirmation of positive ways of being in the world, and encouragement toward goodness, beauty, and truth. As a family, we worked hard to consistently narrate a good story to our children about their lives. We would often use affirming language to this end and encourage them to think of how they might own those values for their own lives. For example, we might say, "We believe God created you to be a hero in your lifetime, to be courageous, to bring light and beauty into the world. We can teach you those things, but you are the one who determines what kind of life you will live. You must choose to follow goodness. To live into the unique design and capacity God has given you, you must choose to practice goodness and learn to listen to the voice of the Holy Spirit."

We referred to this as "will-training," teaching our children that they have the innate ability to grow strong inside and outside and to develop their own self-discipline by the choices they make over time. Again, our goal was to reach hearts, not just to exact moralistic behavior through enforcement. We wanted their behavior to flow out of the vision for life we had helped them develop.

It is important to add here that a child cannot live according to a standard they do not understand. It is imperative that if we want our children to adhere to certain sorts of standards, we must provide those *ahead* of moments of discipline, not only in the instance in which they occur. For instance, whenever we would go over to someone's house, in the car ride over, we would review good principles of what we expected for them in mixed company. If we hadn't helped them understand ahead of time, we felt it was as much our fault as theirs for any aberrant behavior.

Early in our children's lives, Clay wrote a discipleship devotional tool called *Our 24 Family Ways* to help our children understand the particular ways of wisdom we would follow in our own home. The book has, over time, become a tool for many families to use in their own fellowship; but for us, it was a simple way of providing clear parameters for behavior so that our children could know what to expect in unfamiliar settings.

We applied such principles in many settings, from visiting other families, to eating out, to going to church. Here are two examples of what we might say to prepare them:

1. "When we go into Mrs. Brown's house, let's be respectful of her children's toys, just like you would want visitors to our home to be respectful of your belongings. And since this family prepared us a special meal, let's all be sure to thank them for inviting us."

2. "Today in church, let's remember to use our quiet voices so that we can ponder the great thoughts we might hear about God."

No matter the setting, we saw it as an opportunity to shape, to train, and to empower our children to own their choices and develop good habits.

While this active approach to relational training is essential, it is equally important to be able to develop in ourselves the virtue of *discernment*, to know when a child needs to be trained and when a child is simply expressing the more pressing limits placed upon their physical, emotional, and psychological capacities. More often than not, a child doesn't need to be corrected; they need to be comforted, or given a nap, or fed. Sometimes, a child is acting out because we've not provided them with the consistency or provision they need in a given moment; and when that happens, we should not make them feel guilty for something beyond their ability to control.

Note that the first few years of a child's life will require an especially involved and constant attention. Those are the moments when they first engage with their siblings and parents in relationship and where they learn to adapt to daily chores like cleaning up, helping set the table, or unloading the dishwasher. These may seem like frustratingly menial preoccupations in those early years, but I have read and heard it said many times that what is laid as a foundation in the first several years of a child's life will stay with them throughout their life.

And just as your children are learning the basics of virtuous living in the beginning stages of life, by faithfully investing your energy and time in those first few years, you are developing your own muscles of training that you can put to use more readily and easily for the remainder of your life as a parent. Discipline is a long-term process of training, loving, and leading a child to know what and how to think about their life. It is a process, a journey of encountering and embracing goodness over many years. Training our children and learning to be sensitive to their unique responses to our instruction shapes both them and us and calls us all to be our best selves as models of God's truth and grace. The more we seek what the heart of Jesus was in relationship to His disciples, the stronger we grow as parents in the mentoring process of our children

Nathan tells me a story about his teen years when he started spending time with some really foolish companions. He had met them at a class in early college courses and started hanging out with them at church. Despite the worrisome company he was keeping, his trust in us was predicated upon our attention and unconditional love of him and the willingness to understand what he was feeling and thinking that we had developed with him from birth. He didn't always make wise decisions, but he always looked to us for wisdom and advice because we had cultivated such a strong personal relationship of love and affirmation with him. No matter what situation he was in, whether with an immature set of friends or beyond, there was never a moment he felt like he couldn't call us.

Our other children had a few bumps and challenges along the way to adulthood as well. That is completely normal and common as teens learn to manage more of their own responsibility and decisions. And yet somehow, by God's grace, as we pushed through each difficulty, we came out on the other side with trust, close friendship, and grace for each other, covering over both their flaws and ours as parents.

Discipline is a moment-by-moment process over many years of shaping a child's values, faith, and virtue. There are no set rules or guidelines by which to assure a given outcome, but God calls us to be in relationship with our children just as He seeks relationship with us. A couple of our children were rule keepers, and we responded to them according to their personalities. A couple of our children were what we called "spicy," with more outspoken opinions and with more challenges; but with all of the varying personalities, we maintained our close relationship. If we can learn to embrace the improvisatory adventure of relational child training, we will watch our children gain a deeper sense of our love and come to understand that the way we love them is a sign of God's love as well.

From Nathan:

I sulked into my room, slamming the door behind me. I climbed into my bunk bed, buried my face in my pillow, and let out a muffled cry of desperation. I was holding a ball of knots and anger in my stomach that worked its way up my chest and behind my eyes where it began to push out frustrated tears. It had been one of those days that proved to just be too much for my nine-year-old heart. After struggling to understand my school lessons, getting a lecture for not sitting still during reading time, having my friend's mom cancel our playdate, and having my sister get to the last cookie before me, I had found myself with a build-up of pressure that was nearing a pop. While trivial problems in hindsight, they felt very large and very real to my young brain and heart. By the time dinner rolled around, I was nearly bursting with childhood exasperation that was suddenly released with a bang as my sister accidentally kicked my leg beneath the table.

"STOP IT!" I suddenly yelled.

She did stop, and so did the entire table. Every one of my family's eyes were on me, a young boy red with anger and frustration.

"Nathan, we do *not* yell at the table. Do you think you can settle down and tell me in a calm voice what is going on, or would you like to have a few minutes away in your bedroom to rest and settle down a bit? Your choice," my mom said, unsure of what exactly had prompted the sudden and emotional outburst and trying to respond to me with as much grace as she could find in her heart.

"*Fine,* I'll go to my room. You all *suck* anyway!" I said with one last burst of emotion, as I whipped myself out of my chair, and ran across the kitchen, down the stairs, and into my room.

Lying in my bed, I felt a sudden realization of impending doom. I had done it now. Not only had I yelled at my sibling, but I had used a forbidden word. *Suck.* I wasn't trying to be bad, but the circumstances of life had seemed to conspire against me and pushed me to this place. I knew I was in trouble. My parents placed a high value on using words constructively, and generally discouraged anger-filled outbursts at family members. So, I waited, the doom hanging over me, closing in more and more each minute. I waited for my door to be opened, when I would surely be faced with my indiscretions and pay the penalty: a stern talking-to and the seizure of something I really liked. I listened to the footsteps of my family above me and followed their sounds across the ceiling to the stairwell where I then heard my father's heavy footsteps descend the stairs to my door. It opened, my dad came in, and I tried reading his face to gauge how bad the sentencing would be. He sat down on the edge of my bed, and to my surprise, there was no chastising of my bad behavior, no stern warnings, or ultimatums.

Instead, he looked at me and asked, "You seem upset, what's going on?"

All my fears about the punishment I had coming were immediately dispelled. And for the next ten minutes I told my dad my frustrations with the awful day I had experienced. He listened and nodded, and then, when I came to the end of my monologue, he said he understood, at which point the stress ball in my stomach disappeared. Sharing with me that he had many days like that, even now as an adult, was accompanied by a pat on my arm.

He went on to say he had been wanting to spend some more time together, how he wanted to help me make strides toward controlling my emotions. And that I needed to tell my sister I was sorry for yelling at her. Then, he invited me back upstairs to rejoin the family, a new boy, slate wiped clean.

———————

There was a period during my early childhood, in the early nineties, when several books about discipline made their way around the churches my parents attended. In these books, the authors spoke about the proper and godly way to discipline children. They encouraged corporal punishment (spanking) as the right and only way to "train up" a child. They used verses like Proverbs 22:15 that says, "Folly is bound up in the heart of a child, but the rod of discipline will drive it far away"; or old adages like "spare the rod, spoil the child" as evidence that the only way to effectively discipline and train your children was to hit them.

My parents, still in their early years of family life, tried to understand and look for the logic in that line of thinking, but something felt off. They couldn't shake the feeling that hitting their children, for . . . well . . . being children, couldn't be the way to reach their hearts. And it certainly wasn't the logical way Christ would want parents to treat their precious child. So, my father began a biblical search, not only into what the Bible says about discipline, but also how God disciplined His children throughout Scripture.

Through his research, my dad concluded that on both a psychological and spiritual level, spanking or hitting children wasn't only an inferior discipline method but also that it was wrong. He looked to the character of God who, throughout Scripture, is shown and described as endlessly loving, forgiving, and constantly engaging relationally with His loved ones to bring about restoration to His fallen children. This was a far cry from the view of the popular religious crowd who assured parents they only need spank their kids to raise them well.

Aside from searching for the scriptural precedent, my father also looked at the real world of practical and psychological effects of disciplinary methods and found the studies that pointed to the damage that can be done in resorting to corporal punishment. He found that harsh, physical punishment ultimately teaches children that violence is an acceptable reaction to human mistakes, they should be fearful of their parents, and if they make a mistake, they should feel the need to hide it from the people who were designed to help and support them.

So, my dad decided to take his research and study and write it into a book called *Heartfelt Discipline*. The book focused on the felt needs of children for relationship and instruction in their raising, not reactionary violence. As a result of my parents' implementation of this philosophy of discipline, each of us kids walked through childhood, our teenage years, and even adulthood with a strong relationship with our parents intact. That sense of relationship made it possible for us to come to our parents with any mistake we might make throughout our lives and find not reactionary anger but instead guidance, boundaries, and wisdom in a way that actually affected our lives and the people we became.

This theory my father formulated was proven effective when I was in my teens and found myself at a high school party when something terrible happened. I knew I shouldn't have been there; high school kids with no supervision is almost always a recipe for disaster. But even while knowing better, I was in the throes of teenage idiocy, and more than anything, I wanted to be cool. All was seemingly fine until the worst happened: one of the teens drank a bottle of cough medicine and suddenly had a bad reaction to the point that he couldn't speak. All the other teens started going into panic mode—they couldn't call their parents lest they get in trouble, and calling the authorities was out of the question.

As I faced the stressful situation, my heart suddenly calmed as I realized I could call my parents. Would I face some consequences? Maybe, but they had built a relationship with me of trust and connection over seventeen years, one that assured me in that moment they would be on my side, not reactively punishing me and shaming me for an understandable youthful mistake, but instead ready to help and guide me into a healthy and safe outcome for the teen in trouble. As a result of their decision to build that relationship, I was able to fearlessly bring much needed wisdom and insight to the troubled situation that created a better ending to what could have been a catastrophic evening. That relationship was something I'd find myself relying on both in my adolescence and all the way through adulthood.

———

Every child is built entirely differently, which means when it comes to discipline every child will need a unique and tailored approach to their training. Just spanking, or yelling, or grounding is a one-size-fits-all answer that won't ultimately address the training needs a kid has. But many parents worry that without these actions being taken, they'll be left with an ineffective method of discipline that has no lasting effect to curb negative behavior. When practiced with intention and wisdom, leaning into a relational model that includes connection, boundaries, empathy, and instruction will enable parents to see every child's unique needs when it comes to addressing their actions.

The one size fits all approach of spanking and retributive reactivity have been shown to work against the goal of training a child.[1] This type of punishment has been shown to create more aggression and acting out the more it is implemented as a solution to a child's negative behavior. Aside from reactive anger and physical violence breaking a child's trust, sense of safety, and creating a relationship of fear, spanking and anger does nothing to address the unique training needs of every child. If God's chosen method of discipline of us, His children, is one of grace and understanding, why would we think one opposite to that would ever work?

Not only is physical punishment detrimental, but passivity is even worse. When a parent neglects to train a child, give direction, and lead by modeling a virtuous life, the child can feel desperately rejected and act out in many ways. The middle road of relationship, training, and shaping offers the most biblical and foundational flourishing approach.

———

Each of my siblings and I had different needs at different times for discipline. Sometimes it was more boundaries, sometimes it was somber wisdom, and sometimes it was simply a listening ear. As my parents fostered a relationship with each of us, they came to understand what made each of us tick, so that when something went wrong, they could more accurately address the problem and correct it, instead of banging against something and hoping it would suddenly work.

There were times when my rebellion needed to be met head-on as I tested boundaries growing up; this would result in needing a parent to draw clearer boundaries and stand up to my strength. Other times when I would act out, it was from a place of deep frustration of being a growing kid struggling with mental illness; that would require a response of empathy and soothing words. And sometimes I wasn't trying to be "bad" at all, and my destructive behavior came from a place of ignorance, extraversion, and a need to constantly verbally process. This required someone to sit and talk with me, giving me a perspective I hadn't had before. But because my parents both knew me on a deep level and had done the work of creating a relationship of trust and goodness, no matter what situation arose they had the insight into me which gave them wisdom on the most effective way to respond.

This method of relational discipline isn't only practically useful, but it reflects the way God disciplines all of us: in relationship, motivated by love instead of reactionary anger, and informed with personal insight.

In Proverbs 3:11–12 NLT we read this:

> My child, don't reject the LORD's discipline,
>   and don't be upset when he corrects you.
> For the LORD corrects those he loves,
>   just as a father corrects a child in whom he delights.

In the first verse, we see that God *does* discipline, but that He doesn't leave His children to their own devices, letting them figure it out on their own as they hurt themselves and others. He steps in and corrects, guides, and helps. But the way He does it is where we find the "how" in His approach. The second verse reminds us that He "corrects those he loves," evidence that there's a relationship present with the ones He disciplines. The verse is finished with detailing that God disciplines the children He delights in.

So, discipline, while often sounding like a dark and harsh word, when seen in the context of how God uses it, suddenly becomes a beautiful concept where, out of a relational connection, wise guidance, and love, comes a renewed heart and a restored person.

Every one of your children will have vastly different discipline needs at different times. Through building a relationship with them, acting out of love toward them, and using wisdom with them, you can be sure to address each of their unique discipline needs as they grow into the people God has created them to be.

Scripture Reading

Children, obey your parents in the Lord, for this is right. "Honor your father and mother"—which is the first commandment with a promise—"so that it may go well with you and that you may enjoy long life on the earth." Fathers, do not exasperate your children; instead, bring them up in the training and instruction of the Lord. (Ephesians 6:1–4)

FAMILY DISCUSSION QUESTIONS

1. What is the hardest part of being disciplined?

2. When do you feel you are most open to instruction?

3. What is the most helpful way for someone to discipline you?

4. What are ways you could change how you discipline to achieve more positive and constructive outcomes?

5. What's a time you can remember being glad you were disciplined?

ANYTHING THAT'S HUMAN IS
MENTIONABLE, AND ANYTHING
THAT IS MENTIONABLE CAN
BE MORE MANAGEABLE.
WHEN WE CAN TALK ABOUT
OUR FEELINGS, THEY BECOME
LESS OVERWHELMING, LESS
UPSETTING, AND LESS SCARY.

FRED ROGERS

CHAPTER SEVEN

Outside-the-Box Minds

Dear Sally and Nathan,

I'm writing today about my youngest daughter of three precious children. She just turned eleven years old, and as much as my husband and I love her, we are simply at the end of our rope with knowing what to do. Our first two kids were normal as kids go, of course with their own issues, but then came Hannah. From the beginning, Hannah was different. She cried loudly as a baby and never settled. During her toddler years, she struggled with both separation anxiety and a never-ending supply of energy, and sometimes aggression. Now as a pre-teen, Hannah's behavior is a total mystery. She's so smart but struggles greatly in school. While she's lively and funny, she's also unbelievably argumentative and stubborn, starting fights with her siblings and fighting us at every turn. She has an incredibly difficult time focusing, particularly on schoolwork. But most difficult of all, her moods and emotions are entirely unpredictable. We've taken her to get tested, and while no official diagnosis has been made, it seems there's a good chance she has some serious learning disabilities and personality disorders. The professional even indicated she could be on the spectrum. We love her so much, but her personality and needs are eating up so much of our time and energy, and we are suddenly finding ourselves at a loss for what to do.

—Anne

From Sally:

Late one evening, one of my children (seven years old at the time), slipped quietly into our bedroom and gently tapped on my shoulder to awaken me.

"Mama, I really need to talk with you. Can you come and be with me for a while?"

The request was spoken with a steady voice, and yet there was an urgency in it that caught my attention.

I blinked my sleepy eyes, willing them to open, and carefully crawled out of bed so as not to wake up Clay. I went downstairs to the living room, turned on a lamp, and asked, "What is on your heart, sweets?"

"I have some terrible things running around in my mind, and I can't get rid of them. I just can't keep them to myself anymore."

And then, for the next ten minutes, my precious, beloved child poured out frightening and violent thoughts and dreams that had played over and over in their mind every night. A dark cloud of panic moved over my fearful mind. Where did these vicious thoughts come from? Had my child been abused? We had always done our best to protect our children, to help them enjoy their innocence for as long as possible. What had I done to allow such horrifying thoughts to violate the mind of one so vulnerable?

Little could I have known that this would be the first of many instances in which this child would come to me with their troubling thoughts. Every time it happened, I would do my best to pray for wisdom in the midst of my worry and seek whatever guidance and input I could find. But this was long before anyone was really talking openly about mental illness or spectrum issues (e.g., obsessive-compulsive disorder, separation anxiety disorder, panic disorder, and phobias), and I often found myself at a loss because of my lack of information.

Along the way, another child, seemingly "normal," would have occasional bursts of anxiety. We hosted conferences in large hotels across the US, and this child had an irrational fear of elevators and heights, often having trouble sleeping on the top floor suites we were assigned by hotel staff during our events.

And then there was Nathan. From the time he was eighteen months old, his issues were manifest in a multitude of ways. Once, I bought him a pair of darling sneakers with shoestrings. Every day when I helped him put them on, he would fight me, scream, and cry. What a mystery those shoes became! One day, I accidentally tied the shoestrings exactly even on both shoes. I was astonished when, instead of wailing at me, he looked up and smiled. "Oh, tank you, Mama. Dat's right." I realized in an instant that he felt an unquenchable need for the shoelaces to be exactly the same length. At that point, I had never even heard the phrase "obsessive-compulsive" in my life; but I started to make connections through observation, attempting to discern what was going on in his mind.

As I would soon find, each of my children had their own unique mental health issues, all expressed in completely different ways. What started as curious observation became a life of study and desire to understand that has continued to the present day. I realized very quickly that our children weren't trying to rebel against us; instead, their behavior communicated something about their inner workings. I also learned that many mental illnesses are hereditary. This explained some of the behavior of people in our own families.

I did my best to begin to understand what was behind the first layer of expression. I learned early on not to look at their issues as problems of behavior to be fixed, but to peel back initial behavioral reactions and look for the deeper meaning underneath. The more

I did this, the more I was able to see that in many instances, a child may have wanted to obey but was dealing with mental parameters that worked actively against them. Most important, I saw that each of my children was a work of the artist God and that in loving and caring for them, I was taking seriously my stewardship to honor God with the real human beings He had entrusted into my hands. I learned that each, as they were, were complete and a treasure to God. So, accepting and embracing them with unconditional love was a sort of service of worship to Him.

Parenting is challenging, mysterious, and exhausting at times. Often, I would wonder, *Am I failing my children? Is their erratic behavior my fault?* I knew, even as a young mom, that multiple of my children were "different" kids, outside the box of normal behavior and development. For example, certain foods were a trigger for one child's OCD, and elevators, extreme heights, or danger triggered another. And yet it took years of reading, researching, and praying to understand the real triggers for their irregular behavior and what they expressed.

There is so much more information available now to discern and identify foundational issues with unconventional children, but like so many parents in that time, I did the best I was able with the resources I had access to in the moment. Even when I had many more resources later on, it could still take years to really get to the bottom of an issue. I eventually realized that it would require me to embrace the mystery of my children and to learn to love them in their complexity. It was a sign of my affirmation that the relationships in our family were built on a foundation of unconditional love. Instead of trying to fix them, over time, I learned to read their moods and be patient with them in their anger and inability to control their triggers. The fact that we had more than one outside-the-box child helped my other children grow strong in patience and acceptance of "unique" people in our lives.

There is no doubt that children with mental health issues or who are on the spectrum can be very trying. And my children were indeed a mystery and difficulty for Clay and me countless times. Even answers and diagnoses—which, in the moment, can feel so reassuring—don't really "solve" the problems. If we expect our children with these issues simply to get better, we are preparing ourselves, and them, for a lot of disappointment. There are rarely "fixable" solutions. But gaining wisdom from medical knowledge and communities of people who share the same conditions has empowered both my children and me and given us ways of moving forward.

Over time, we have all matured and grown more adept at making space for each other, especially in being attentive to environments that are more protected against triggers. An abundance of communication, a willingness to understand, no small dose of patience, and unyielding love has breathed life into our lives and helped each unique child know that they are seen, understood, and valued no matter the circumstances. We also have been shaped into a more compassionate and sympathetic family toward others who have difficulties in their lives.

Beyond the purview of family, there are other potential areas of challenge. Many wonderful friends and family, speaking with nothing but the best of intentions, have offered formulaic solutions to our children's behavioral issues related to their diagnoses.

"If you are stricter and sterner with them, they'll respond to you."

"You're probably just feeding them too much sugar."

"Maybe *you're* just having a hormonal day!"

Outside the initial heat I felt rising in those moments, I can see that such friends and family members are generally well-intentioned; and yet I have often walked away from such conversations feeling guilty, as if perhaps it *is* my fault that my children can't just overcome these issues. It was in reading books about mental illness and meeting others with children like mine that I began to feel more understood, like I had a community of others around me who had experienced what I had. Walking through mental illness in a child can be a day-to-day process and feel relentless at times. Learning to find outlets for peace and affirmation is essential for making it in the long run.

Accepting the ramifications of my children's challenges has helped me learn to be content over time. I know now that there simply isn't a quick fix; but God chose me to be the mother for these children. I trusted that He would also give me the wisdom and ability to shepherd them through these issues. My journey with mental illness has involved radical acceptance of my children's lives, and an awareness that every day might be filled with new surprises and interruptions.

There are no perfect children or perfect parents. There is only the invitation to embrace a life of walking with open hands and a willingness to grow a bit more every day, in spite of setbacks. That is where we encounter God's grace at work in the most complicated moments of our lives, taking our complexities and weaving them into something beautiful.

From Nathan:

I watched the suburbs pass by in the window as I processed the previous hour. The normality of the fast-food drive-throughs and neighborhood houses that flew by on the outside seemed to contradict the monumental and life-changing thing that was happening inside my mind and heart. My mom kept looking over at me, putting her hand on my shoulder at stoplights. I was fifteen, and we were driving home after an appointment with a psychotherapist who had just diagnosed me for the first time.

For years, I, and everyone around me, knew I was different; they could see it in how I behaved and moved through the world. I could feel it in every thought and emotion I had ever had. For years, I had felt like I was "too much" and "not enough" all at once. I would see kids in class as they easily grasped school lessons while I, trying to understand, was consistently yelled at by teachers. I watched my siblings who were able to sit still and read a book, while my eyes darted around the room and mixed up the words, and my foot tapped on the floor, my body unable to contain the boundless energy that needed a way out.

I watched as almost everyone easily carried on with their lives completely uninhibited by the compulsions that lived so presently in my mind, pushing me to constantly wash my hands, take showers, and fear touching people. I wanted to be "normal," to be accepted and just go through life without feeling "other"; but no matter how hard I tried, I found myself interacting with life like an animal at the zoo, staring through the glass at all the normal people who got to live normal lives with normal minds, while mine seemed to have waged war with me for as long as I can remember.

We pulled into our driveway, but my mom didn't get out. I turned to look at her.

"What are you feeling right now?" she asked.

I thought but didn't say, *Taking inventory of what the professional said about me and what it means about who I am.* Part of me felt relieved. For years, I had thought I was just messed up, that God had made a mistake or used faulty parts when putting me together. But to hear that my behaviors, proclivities, and patterns had names, and that other people had them too, meant I wasn't as weird as I thought; that somewhere out there, there were others like me who had maybe experienced the same struggles and pain I had been dealing with my entire life.

But I also felt hopeless because these things that had caused so much difficulty and frustration in my young life were here to stay. The thought of dealing with these "disorders" forever made me suddenly hopeless and tired.

"I don't know," I finally answered, unusually unsure of how to put the large number of complicated thoughts into words.

We sat there in the silence, me trying to find words that would fully capture the depth of what I was thinking and feeling, and my mom trying to know what to say to her troubled son. Through the front window of our house, I could see my siblings sitting on the couch reading quietly. I suddenly envied them and thought a prayer to God, *Why couldn't I just be normal like them? Why did you let this happen to me?*

Then suddenly, I felt a hand on my shoulder, I turned to see my mom looking me in the eye and knowing, without a word, the inner war that was waging inside me. She looked at me and smiled in a way only moms can do before saying this:

"Nathan, I'm so glad you're my son. You are the most amazing kid in the world. You have boundless creativity, a loving heart, and a deep and beautiful mind. I know it must be confusing, maybe even scary right now. But now that we know what you're dealing with, we can figure out a way forward together. You aren't messed up. Your mind isn't messed up—it's amazing and perfectly designed by God. It just needs a little help. I love you."

I let her words sink in, and suddenly felt less alone, less troubled, and more hopeful. To hear that even in the midst of these diagnoses and the difficulty I had had since I was born didn't make me bad, or messed up, and perhaps they were even part of what made me great was a salve to my mind and soul.

We exited the car and walked into a journey we took together of seeing my mind as a beautiful and unique creation that needed special attention and putting the puzzle pieces together of how I was going to use it to tell the story God had for me.

Approximately 20 percent of American children ages three to seventeen have been diagnosed with a mental, emotional, behavioral, or developmental disorder (often accompanied by learning disabilities);[1] and about 17 percent will be diagnosed each year with a developmental disability or "neurodiversity."[2] The numbers are growing every day: we've seen a sharp uptick in the percentages of children with autism and ADHD than in previous years, mainly due to the fact we are now more aware of and quicker to diagnose and seek help for struggling kids.[3] What was once thought of as a fluke or a freak occurrence is now known to be something that will—and is—affecting millions of families in the US and around the world.

Both my family and I always knew I was different; but in getting diagnosed, we suddenly were given the ability to know why and given resources for how to live with it.

But even though great strides have been made in the recognition and action around kids dealing with different kinds of minds and emotions, there are still many who don't receive the help, support, and resources they need to thrive into their adult lives. Research shows that nearly half of all suicides are from individuals who had a known mental health condition.[4]

I've heard stories from adults who were told they were "bad" or "lazy" or "dumb" when they were kids and learned later that they were actually dealing with a mental illness, learning disability, or neurodiverse condition. Because of this, they endured years of pain that isolated them from people and things they loved and gave them a self-image of being broken, an image they will spend the rest of their lives trying to heal from or worse.

But there's hope. There's hope in God's plan and in recognizing when our child needs help. My mom didn't assume I was bad, or lazy, or dumb. She knew better because she knew me. And she believed that God had entrusted me to her to help and guide and love no matter what that might entail. She always knew I was different; from an early age I displayed behavior that wasn't "normal." And when puberty hit, my differences grew even larger. My mom, knowing me and listening to God, took even more focused and proactive action to address my needs.

Every kid will have unique needs that must be addressed with love. They might not fall under the terms of mental illness, learning disabilities, or neurodiversity, but many will display behavior that falls outside what the world thinks is normal, and they will need special attention. It's in looking at your kids, evaluating their needs, even the difficult ones, that you as parents have one of two choices:

1. Treating your child and their high maintenance needs as a curse. Comparing them to other kids and the image of what you (and the world) think is normal. Imposing the idea of who they "should be" on them, then vacillating between unrealistic expectations of them and exasperation when they fail to meet them. Treating your child as a problem and their needs as impositions.

OR

2. Celebrating your child and the amazingly unique creation they are. Finding the good and beautiful things about them even in the midst of their more difficult attributes. Stepping into the frustration they face as a result of their differences.

Walking with them through the hard parts of themselves and empowering the great parts of who they are.

The first one is a natural human reaction. It's normal to be frustrated and even angry when we come in contact with issues we don't understand or feel we have no control over. But so often the frustration parents feel translates to children that they are "less than," "disappointments," or "messed up," ultimately affecting their self-image (even into adulthood) and adding external pain to the internal wars they are waging. This reaction is understandable but also destructive to the heart of any child.

The second is a supernatural choice that acts out an understanding of how God looks at us—seeing us as "fearfully and wonderfully" made unique creations, celebrating the beautiful ways we are different, and lovingly helping and guiding us through the difficult parts of ourselves. When parents choose to see their children's needs, not as problems but as possibilities, both the child and the parent benefit from a closer relationship and a shared victory of overcoming together.

This is a long-term journey, and it will require lots of patience. I still struggle to this day as an adult with mental illness, learning disabilities, and controlling my outside-the-box personality and chaotic mind. But in the years that my parents walked with me through my "disorders," I have felt their presence and support in a real way that has enabled me to confidently and securely charge headlong into the story that God has waiting for me.

Raising a child, no matter their differences, can be an ordeal. But it's also a wonderful and beautiful opportunity to shape and empower a soul that has been entrusted into your loving hands. It'll be a long journey (a whole life), but it's a worthy one that will eventually eclipse any troubles you encounter. When you give your child the freedom to embrace their uniquenesses and inspire the vision to see themselves as beautifully designed person, they will begin to understand how they fit into the grand story that God is telling.

Scripture Reading

*You have searched me, L*ORD*,*
  and you know me.
You know when I sit and when I rise;
  you perceive my thoughts from afar.
You discern my going out and my lying down;
  you are familiar with all my ways.
Before a word is on my tongue
  *you, L*ORD*, know it completely.*
You hem me in behind and before,
  and you lay your hand upon me.
Such knowledge is too wonderful for me,
  too lofty for me to attain. (Psalm 139:1–6)

FAMILY DISCUSSION QUESTIONS

1. In what ways do you feel different from other people?

2. What is the hardest thing about being different?

3. What do you love about being different?

4. How can you use your unique attributes (even the ones that are difficult) for good in the world?

5. How do you need support in dealing with your differences?

THINGS ARE NEVER
QUITE AS SCARY
WHEN YOU'VE GOT
A BEST FRIEND.

BILL WATTERSON,
CALVIN AND HOBBS

CHAPTER EIGHT

Friends and Relationships

Dear Sally and Nathan,

My two kids are my entire world. At thirteen and fifteen, they have just entered the stage of life when they are going out there and making friends on their own apart from my oversight and guidance. My girl is a firecracker; we call her "the Pied Piper" as she seems to make friends everywhere she goes and almost always has something to do, someone to see, and a new friend to spend time with. My son, on the other hand, is almost the opposite. He has difficulty forming connections and ends up most days and weekends in his room reading, working on hobbies, and playing video games. We thought this was just the way he was as he seemed content, but we worry he might be missing out on important social developmental at this age. Rather than push him, we decided to talk to him and ask him how he feels. He told us he loves being in his own world, doing the things he loves on his own, but he also ended by saying, it can also get very lonely. Since then, we've tried to help him find friends, but it seems a harder task than we'd hoped. He'll say he wishes he had a friend, but when we encourage him to reach out to someone, he clams up and ends up back in his room. We want him to be himself but also be able to form healthy friendships, and we're unsure how to help. We're not only worried about this for this age, we worry as he gets older he might regret not having some close friends and even might have difficulty finding a spouse. Please help us in knowing how to help him.

—Jamie

From Sally:

With booted feet tromping over cobbled roads, I hurried on my way to a local haunt for a weekly meetup with one of my children. After four years living off and on in Oxford, I've been introduced to many lovely, hidden gems of cafés and restaurants where I have spent many an hour in intimate conversation with various of my children. No matter where our lives have taken us, if we find our paths intersecting for a while in a given place, we make a dedicated effort to spend time together over coffee or a meal as friends. Over time, my friendships with each of my children have only grown more rewarding and valuable. They are growing because we have intentionally invested over the decades.

Somehow, in this instance, the strange meandering roads led my child and me to Oxford, the City of Dreaming Spires; and yet, when we finally arrived and settled in at our table with tea and a scone, our conversation was as familiar as it had been anywhere else in the world.

Even as my children have moved to far-off cities for work or study, I have made it a point each week to phone or arrange video calls to cultivate times of rich conversation, so that I can hear their joys and sorrows, encourage them in their journeys, and express my love. Friendship has been at the heart of all our relationships from the beginning.

As I survey my decades as a mother, I can remember my early years, when I naively thought that all of my children would easily find close friends. Even though our pathway as a family took us through many moves, I always tried to help us quickly get involved in church activities and other support groups wherever we went. Despite my best efforts, there were instances when one or two of my children lacked companions of their own age. Loneliness was simply an unavoidable reality through many moments of our family's history.

This was perhaps compounded by the fact that a couple of our children are simply more solitary by nature, and so would take longer to make friends in new places. I quickly learned that it is impossible to force our children to be friends with anyone if it isn't a natural fit. For a long time, I was beset with the conventional wisdom and advice that said, "It isn't natural for children to be close to their parents; they need to branch out and have friends their own age." Eventually I realized that sometimes such "wisdom" can be reductive if not understood with nuance. I faithfully made myself available during the many twists and turns of each of their lives, and as I look over the past several decades, I can see that each of our friendships was only growing more valuable year after year.

As my children entered their teen years, they pursued friendships and community settings attuned to their expanding borders. And yet, as lived experience often reveals, it was often difficult to find peers whose values, activities, and interests matched a particular child. We live in a disparate time in which the foundations that might once have provided the assurance of mutually held ways of seeing the world, and of a moral framework to follow, have largely crumbled. Now, we are dealing with vastly different views of the world, even from family to family. Add to that the pervasive ways that social media worms its way into the messages both we and our children listen to on a daily basis, and it isn't hard to see why it can be so difficult to find kindred spirits, both for our children and even for us.

At some point along the way, I had an epiphany. I saw that what my children longed for more than anything else is to belong to a community who would celebrate life with them, who could come around them in times of crisis, and who could celebrate their victories. I felt especially strongly about supporting my children in this way, given that we had shared so little in the ways of regular life or even holidays with extended family. I realized that if my children were to feel accepted and beloved within a group of people, it would be imperative for Clay and me to create our home as a place of belonging.

In past cultural history, communities were much more stable and integrated into a particular place. But in our own time, modern technology and the mobility it has enabled has had an adverse effect on our sense of rootedness in a place or people. Once people knew their neighbors and shared their whole lives and values with them, but that experience is gone from our breathless modern age; many of us don't even know our own neighbors' names. Our churches even reflect this reality, shifting from local parishes and fellowships to megachurch models that encompass vast numbers of people without any sense of the intimacy of shared community. And the transience of culture all but assures that any attempt to find this kind of integrated life again will be very difficult.

As we grappled with this reality ourselves, we decided that even in spite of our sense of loneliness or isolation, we could make our own home a safe harbor of belonging and becoming. We began to develop a sense of home as a place where people could feel welcomed and loved, be invited into a community of loving, like-minded people where they could feel at peace within its walls. And so, Clay and I sought such friendships out. We held regular dinners for families so we could have a sense of shared camaraderie with people of all ages. We hosted teen and adult parties, pizza nights, Christmas scavenger hunts, music evenings, summer barbecues, Christmas teas, birthday bashes, and so much more. We wanted our children to know what it meant to be beloved and to exemplify in our own lives the patterns of love and service that could make that kind of deep friendship possible.

As such, each celebration was focused on cultivating a sense of community, an expanding of the bounds of family to others in love and generosity.

Isolation and loneliness have become a norm in the last decades; this was compounded by the COVID pandemic years and the social separation it necessitated. Disturbingly, suicide rates have increased in nearly every age group.[1] Something has gone terribly wrong in our culture, and at its root are the most human of needs: the need to belong, to be loved, and to be seen. We are designed by God to flourish in relationship. Love and affection are like oxygen to human beings to keep us healthy. No matter our different personalities, all of us are made to be cherished from the start and to be held within the protective net of unconditional love.

As I look at my children in their current lives all over the world, I can see how profoundly different their needs are. As I've discussed in earlier portions of this book, my children differ greatly in their personalities, and their lives have borne those proclivities out in very specific ways. One of them is busy to the hilt with four children and an active writing career; one of them is a quiet artist who needs to retreat from the world and find their artist's voice within; another artist in the family needs more outward engagement and runs both a podcast and an online discussion group; and one has an active speaking and writing career in academia, traveling constantly and engaging with a wide variety of different people. Very different personalities and work choices; and yet even with those varied parameters, I can see that the need for anchored, reliable relationships has never changed. Though all are quite different from each other, all of them share a mutual sense of desiring friendship with each other, being part of the "club of companions" that our family is.

And I recognize my own role in exemplifying that principle as their mother. Even in their adulthood, I continue to be a faithful friend to each of them who cares about the intricate details of their lives—their pressures, finances, relationships, faith growth, and overall heart issues. I keep their secrets and seek to be a "safe" person in whom they can confide. I am determined to continue in that joyful role for my whole life.

Being a friend of adult children has required adapting to a new way of interacting with them. I've learned to accept their unique choices of how to live their life, their clothing choices, the movies they watch, their ways of relating to life, and their faith decisions. I have learned to love them even as I trust them to God and pray that they live their lives well. I have made myself an open conversation partner in hearing them on their individual choices as adults, and as such have become a sounding board for them when they are open to it, a persona of wise counsel if they request it. And in that context, I learn from them as well, benefitting from their stories and enjoying their companionship as it is possible to do so.

It is essential to cultivate deep and abiding friendships with your children. The pathway to liking them and who they are becoming starts during the baby years and blossoms into adulthood. I can tell you from experience that the growth of friendship with your children is a priceless treasure that will fill you with grace for a lifetime.

And so, my child and I had a strong pot of tea, a rousing two-hour discussion, robust laughter, secrets whispered in this very public place, and the "ahhh" moments of taking a break from life. And so was the gift of our close Clarkson community that came from years of cultivation.

From Nathan:

My mom has always endearingly nicknamed me "the Pied Piper," which refers to a fairy tale about a man with a magical flute who was able to play a song that would cause all range of creatures and people to follow him, entranced by his tune. She called me this when she saw as a young child that I had an innate ability to draw people to myself.

From an early age, I displayed the unique ability to connect with all sorts of people and engage in friendships with a variety of individuals. This played out in my organizing the neighborhood kids to gather together and build forts in our backyard, or direct imaginary tales on the playground with a cast of diverse and excited kids. This was all well and good when I was a kid, where my friend group was overseen by my parents' watchful eyes. But then I turned seventeen and had in my possession a driver's license, which expanded my freedom to form friendships beyond their purview.

Suddenly, in high school, I started bringing a barrage of interesting characters through the doors of our home; some were wild, some were weird, some were troubled. I'm sure my parents had more than a few nervous moments of hesitance at the colorful parade of youths. But where my parents could've tried to contain and control me out of fear, limiting my sphere of peers and tamping down my love of people, they instead decided to embrace their son's natural and unique proclivity for connecting with people and making friends of all kinds, even if it fell outside their expectations.

So, instead of making me cut people out of my life, they stayed connected to me relationally and opened our home to all the characters I drew in. They hosted movie nights, made cookies, and even opened themselves up to counsel and befriend the teens I brought through our doors. This enabled me to live out the natural, God-given, unique way I was made to make friends, while they stayed involved enough to guide and provide me wisdom along the way. They didn't try to change the way I was made to make friends and form relationships. Instead, they celebrated and guided it.

Conversely, one of my siblings was almost the complete opposite of me in their methodology of going about forming relationships. They were introverted and moved more carefully when making friends. As a result, this sibling often dealt with loneliness and frustration, wanting to form a few close friendships but also being choosy as to who they let in. This resulted in long bouts of feeling like they were not ever going to make a friend. Like any parent would, mine worried, wanting deeply to help this child not feel the pain of isolation.

My parents could have seen this child as a problem, pressured them to be more like me, to just be more extroverted, friendly, and less choosy, which would've ultimately made them feel that they were defective. But my parents, following God's calling of accepting their children's uniqueness in every way, decided to work with my sibling's unique personality to help and support them in the journey of them having friends. So, they started book clubs at our house around books that coincided with my sibling's particular interest, and they looked far and wide for groups and communities that more specifically were centered around their interests, so their child could connect with friends that were more in line with their particular needs and desires.

Every child needs friends and relationships. This is something that God has woven into their DNA to need and long for. Research shows that friendships in a young child's life have a host of positive and even needed benefits, including: social development, creating a greater capacity for empathy, boosting happiness and self-confidence, and elevating happiness levels, while decreasing stress.[2] Learning to make and maintain friendships is a skill that will not only benefit your child as they grow into adults, but will also make them healthier and more joyful.

We even see Scripture enthusiastically endorse the importance of friendships. Proverbs says this about what having a good friend can add to someone's life:

Perfume and incense bring joy to the heart,
and the pleasantness of a friend
springs from their heartfelt advice. (Proverbs 27:9)

Throughout the Bible, we're given pictures of what good friendships look like and can accomplish. We see the story of the biblical hero David and his friendship with Jonathan, their friendship being a blessing to the future king on his difficult journey as well as a means for saving David's life. We watch the great prophets Elijah and Elisha supporting each other in their callings. We see Ruth and Naomi giving each other strength in grief and hope for the future. We see Paul sharing his troubles and triumphs with companions like Timothy and Barnabas. Then, ultimately, we see Jesus befriending twelve disciples—eating, laughing, talking, and doing ministry together, the results of which changed the entire course of history and accomplished God's will to redeem the world and establish His church.

Friends are an important part of God's plan for us to live out His calling on our lives and find personal health and joy. But which friends each child will need and the way each will go about finding those friends will be entirely unique. And every child will need the help and guidance from their parents on how to accomplish this in a healthy and productive way.

I still remember the endless amounts of tips and guidance my parents gave me as I ventured out to form relationships with kids at Sunday school, classes, and field trips: "Make sure to show interest in them; ask them questions"; and "Be confident! Look them in the eye"; and "Don't be afraid to share your interests; they might find it interesting too!" These bits of advice still ring in my head today, and having practiced and seen the results of my parents' guidance, I still utilize their instruction to form relationships that continue to bless me in my adult life. But all of this is indicative of parents who cared enough to help me along this path.

———

When it comes to helping your children form relationships and foster friendships, you will see that most kids fall into two camps that can be defined by the classic MBTI personality types we're all very familiar with: introverts and extroverts.

Extroverted kids typically have a natural inclination and talent for building connections more often with more people. They tend to have a larger social group and form friendships quickly. This is a wonderful and amazing gift. Where they'll need unique guidance and direction is in learning to discern with whom they ought to form relationships, so as to surround themselves with healthy and positive influences. They'll also need help learning the art of balance, knowing when to take a step back and invest in quiet or alone time, and when to invest more deeply in the friendships they already have before searching for new friends to solidify the bonds that will ultimately serve them in the long-term.

Introverted kids are naturally inclined to spend time on their own and in their own world until they feel comfortable enough to let in someone who they deem worthy. This careful and quiet approach can be beneficial in their lives, but when they're unguided, their approach can turn into overly cautious behavior and leave them feeling very lonely and separated from people around them. They will need special support and encouragement to step out of their comfort zone and interact with people, even when it's difficult and those people don't fit their vision of who could be their friend. They may also need help learning the art of reaching out and knowing others so as to form the connections their hearts so deeply long for.

————

We were all made for connection, but the ways we go about achieving that are unique to our makeup and stories. Helping your child in this journey of connection with others will aid them at every stage of life. Further, all the concepts relating to forming friendships explored above will be relevant once your child looks for a romantic partner and spouse.

No two kids will go about forming friendships the exact same way. But guiding your child, regardless of personality, into the skills of making, keeping, and cultivating friendships will be a blessing to them, and ultimately, a necessity for them to live out God's calling.

Scripture Reading

Two are better than one,
  because they have a good return for their labor:
If either of them falls down,
  one can help the other up.
But pity anyone who falls
  and has no one to help them up.
Also, if two lie down together, they will keep warm.
  But how can one keep warm alone?
Though one may be overpowered,
  two can defend themselves.
A cord of three strands is not quickly broken.
(Ecclesiastes 4:9–12)

FAMILY DISCUSSION QUESTIONS

1. Do you want more friends? Why or why not?

2. Which friendship from a movie or book do you admire?

3. What's the hardest part of either making or having friends?

4. Why do you think having friends is important?

5. What are some ways you could make a friend?

THERE NEEDS TO BE A
HOMEMAKER EXERCISING SOME
MEASURE OF SKILL, IMAGINATION,
CREATIVITY, DESIRE TO FULFILL
NEEDS AND GIVE PLEASURE TO
OTHERS IN THE FAMILY. HOW
PRECIOUS A THING IS THE HUMAN
FAMILY. IS IT NOT WORTH SOME
SACRIFICE IN TIME, ENERGY,
SAFETY, DISCOMFORT, WORK?
DOES ANYTHING COME FORTH
WITHOUT WORK?

EDITH SCHAEFFER

CHAPTER NINE

Lifegiving Community

Dear Sally and Nathan,

I have four children from ages nine to fourteen. I have loved my entire journey of being a mom and raising them well, but in the past couple of years, I've been noticing a lack of familial closeness. I am a new reader of the Clarkson books, but one of the things that immediately drew me in was your family's apparent closeness. I didn't grow up in a close-knit family, but I always wished that I had. When reading about your family traditions and the closeness in both your parent-child and sibling relationships, I experienced a longing for something I wasn't given but that I want to give my children before they leave my home. But I'm at a loss as to how to foster a deeper affection and preference between them as well as between them and me. They mostly get along, but most of the kids have completely full, separate lives from each other, each with their own friend group, activities, and schedules. We've tried to have family dinners, but it's rare all of us are in the same place at the same time, and whenever I try and make it a reality, I get pushback from the kids who want to live their own lives. I only have a little more time to make this a reality and just don't know how to make space for deep and close relationships to form between them and all of us, but I desperately wish I knew how. Could you help me understand what it is I need to do to give my children a true sense of familial community?

—Jennifer

From Sally:

As my children entered their mid-teen years and began to strain toward adulthood, each expressed a desire to have some independence and spread their wings a bit. We recognized this need even as we saw that the culture around them exemplified a sexual promiscuity and liberation from moral behavior that often diametrically opposed the moral framework we had attempted to offer our children.

Once a child begins that transition toward their full adult life, it is only natural that they look to others to validate their changing experience of the world and the new ways they are inhabiting it. I knew that as much as I longed for our children to hold fast to the values we had instilled in them, they would need more than just Clay and me to affirm a biblical worldview. They would need to see others they respected held the same dedication to a Christ-centered life.

As it happened, both The Chronicles of Narnia and The Lord of the Rings started releasing in theaters as my children began to hit their pivotal later teen years. Our kids all loved the books and were excited for the release of the films, and Clay and I even attended the midnight releases of several of the movies with our children as a special celebration and in support of this interest.

Along the way, one of my children asked me if I would want to save up with her to attend a C. S. Lewis conference in Oxford. We decided it would be an amazing opportunity for us to immerse ourselves inside the world of Lewis, J. R. R. Tolkien, and other "Inklings" authors so dear to our family. For about ten days one summer, the two of us walked the cobbled streets of Oxford, attending lectures, visiting Lewis's home, and enjoying tea times with other enthusiasts of these two great authors. And so began our family devotion to all things Oxford.

During our time there, we visited a pub called The Eagle and Child, where Lewis and Tolkien met regularly with a group of other writing friends. The group, colloquially referred to by its members as "the Inklings," provided many years of comradeship for all involved, and an open forum to discuss ideas and share lives. Both Lewis and Tolkien would later recount that the shared fellowship, and the input they received about their own writing from others in the group, profoundly influenced their stories, beloved by countless people around the world. The community of friends met from approximately 1931 to 1949, and together they experienced the joy of companionship, from long hikes to joyful shared meals. While the group shifted and changed some over the years, the core group remained together for the duration.

As we sat in The Eagle and Child, drinking sparkling cider and listening to the many stories of their experiences together, I gained a renewed vision for just how community might help friends and family members hold fast to their faith and keep their virtues alive over many years. When I went back home to my family, I rededicated myself to implementing many of the ideas we had encountered in Oxford to our home community, seeking to provide fellowship for each of my four children in ways that would give them the grace and joy of solidarity with like-minded peers with whom they could share their ideals.

I applied this especially in the direction of the friendships my children were developing beyond our home. I realized that I would rather go to the trouble of hosting—effectively, incentivizing our children's friends to come to our home—because then we could encourage not only our own children but also give life and light to others as well, all the while keeping a weather eye on what was going on in our kids' respective worlds. Over the years, we cultivated many opportunities for fellowship.

One idea was a Christmas scavenger hunt, where older teens would team up with a carful of friends and take photos with their phones of assigned landmarks nearby: a snowman, a home with white Christmas lights, a cappuccino coffee from a local cafe, or the whole group in front of a Christmas tree.

Another effort was to borrow directly from Lewis and Tolkien and start an "Inklings" group from among one of my children's friend group. I was delighted to discover small, individual sparkling apple juice bottles, which we dubbed "English ale," and I made cottage pie for their shared mealtimes. The group shared their creative work with each other—from original stories to paintings from budding artists and new compositions played on the guitar or piano. Little by little, the group bonded through these experiences and became the closest of friends.

Of course, there were countless other ways to implement such communal activities. I remember teaching a group of Nathan's friends how to make chicken cordon bleu so that they could host some of their girlfriends in a formal dinner in our house. I'll never forget when one of the "dudes" threw a chicken breast across the room to a friend and said, "Heads up! Chicken coming your way!" Those meals, and many beyond, drew Nathan's friends into our home, giving me a chance to know some of his buddies, and in turn, to understand Nathan more and affirm him. And we hosted countless dinners like that for our kids' friends, from cookouts on our deck, to pizza and movie nights.

During Christmas one year, I instituted a progressive dinner with a group of other families, starting in one home for appetizers, driving to another family's home for a main course, and ending up at the final destination for desserts and hot drinks. The experience made for a rousing time of feasting, fellowship, games, and cherished memories for all, and we carried on the tradition with that same group for many years after.

One of our most important community rhythms as a family has centered around our Sunday teatime. Ever since the kids were toddlers, we have gathered in our living room on Sunday afternoon with a strong pot of piping hot tea and a scrumptious treat. We light candles, put on background music, and share a moment of Sabbath fellowship. Even today, whether we are together or spread to the four winds, we all celebrate our Sunday teatimes wherever we are around the world.

Personally, I've delighted in the many Bible studies I've hosted for countless women in my home. It became part of the natural breathing patterns that our children experienced in our family. And Clay and I applied our experience of organizing those home groups to our own conferences, which we hosted for countless women over two decades. Our children came with us to our events and contributed as part of the staff, meeting attendees, speaking and singing from the stage, participating in staff prayer times, and joining in a celebratory feast at the end of each conference with our whole team.

While many of these efforts toward community were often made without a clear sense of how they were affecting our children, there were moments where the impact was made clear to me. In more recent years, I was sitting in my candlelit living room late in the evening, sharing a best friend conversation with one of my adult children. As we spoke, they opened up to me about the richness of our family community.

"You know, Mama, so many situations I encountered out in the world made me question my beliefs, tore at my convictions, and cast a shadow over all that I had been taught to believe in our home. But as I look back now, I can see that the strong community you developed for us, of friends with like-minded ideals, ingrained deep within me the unwavering belief that our faith was not just unique to us, but shared by many people. I knew, no matter what confusion I experienced, that I *wasn't alone*. I can see now how much effort it took for you and Dad, from hosting, to cooking meals, to cleaning up the messes we left afterward. I want you to know it was worth it. By cultivating that sense of shared fellowship and guiding our whole group into patterns of faith and love, you created a sort of positive peer pressure that helped us know that we had a group to whom we belonged, that we weren't the only ones who held fast to our faith. They, and you, were a 'cloud of witnesses' to me in moments when I might otherwise have felt isolated and alone."

Not all of our attempts to build community worked, and even when they did, some lasted longer than others. And yet we kept our eyes alert for people of faith and virtue, and we found them sprinkled into our lives in such a way that we felt the strength of fellow comrades-in-arms through many years.

And at the heart of it all, it was our own family community— the Clarkson six—that became the most crucial fellowship of all. It was, and continues to be, in our little familial congregation that our children have come to find the friendship and support they need. It is a camaraderie developed over many years of repeated patterns of affirming our belonging to each other that we all represent a shared haven of rest and peace for each other. We support one another, encourage each other, and act as anchors holding each other in place in a chaotic world.

Do we fuss from time to time? Of course! Have we done everything to perfection? Certainly not. And yet, our imperfect community, constructed in love, is how we have found the strength to thrive over many years. Now, to that community, we have added new spouses and grandchildren, who have all found their own place as beloved in our dedicated group. From this ember of our shared communion, the love of Christ grows outward to encompass more and more into its unique fold.

From Nathan:

Once a year for over thirty years now, my family has held something called "Family Day." This day is celebrated with as much intention, excitement, and recognition as Christmas or Thanksgiving. With every special day or holiday, there is a special intention, a focus of the day; Family Day is no different. Family Day is a day in late summer where we spend one day with each other celebrating all of us individually and as a group. It's a day we celebrate what makes us, us.

The day starts with the whole family gathering around a breakfast meal of homemade cinnamon rolls, scrambled eggs, bacon, and lots of coffee where we laugh, eat, and set a mood of joy for the coming hours. Following the breakfast feast, we all head to the kitchen where we help my mother prepare the next feast of the day, all of us running to and fro with spatulas and ingredients. Once the meal is prepared, we pack it into a giant blue cooler. Then all of us, along with the cooler, pile into one minivan and we begin a journey, a short road trip.

On the way, we each get a turn to play our choice of beloved songs that we all sing with each other at the top of our lungs while watching the countryside pass by. We drive and sing and laugh until we arrive at our destination, usually about an hour from our home. The destination has changed throughout the years, depending on where we've lived at the time, but it is always chosen with care. It has to be a place away from the world—a mountain lookout, an oceanside beach, a state park—and away from the normalcy of our everyday life that serves as a unique and beautiful backdrop for memories.

Once we arrive, spilling out of the car, we begin to explore, hike, and recognize the beauty of God's creation that holds us and dwells among us. Then after we are thoroughly out of breath, we eat (again) another feast of homemade fried chicken that we kids "helped" Mom make. Once our stomachs are full, it is time to cement the memory with the family photoshoot. This part can take hours, wrangling four adult children (and now in-laws and grandchildren) into position, finding the right view, and a having a million outtake pictures as the result of too much giggling. Once we get the shot, we head home. But the day isn't over yet.

Then comes the most important part of Family Day, "the re-membering." Once we get home and rest for a while, we all come back together and gather in our aptly named "living room" where my dad pulls out an enormous folder filled with the records of Family Days past. With a pen in his hand and blank paper ready, we each go around the room and talk about what we're thankful for in the past year: new job opportunities, getting into schools, getting married, having children, making friends, chance encounters, good health, and anything in which we can see the hand of God at work.

My dad takes care to write each down carefully. Then we go around again and say our prayer requests for what we are hoping and praying for in the coming year. In keeping this record, we see how uniquely God has and continues to work in the lives of each of us individually and as a family. We also are actively taking part in each other's stories in a way where we can encourage, guide, and cheer on each other in the stories we're each telling. We close with prayers of thanksgiving and petition.

We've celebrated Family Day for over three decades, and as a result, we have seen how God ties all of our unique stories together in a beautiful and long-lasting way. This practice of celebration and observance has both allowed each of us the joy of living our own stories and the privilege of being a part of someone else's.

My siblings are adults now. We all left home years ago and have gone on to live in different parts of the world on multiple continents. We each have different careers we're pursuing and our own unique friend groups and churches. A couple of us have married, one of us has started a family and has kids of their own. We have our own homes, our own people, our own jobs, and our own callings. But even though we are separated by time zones, geography, and the reality of busy lives, we have never drifted relationally.

No matter where we are in the world, we each choose to make time to see each other. My siblings often buy plane tickets to visit me in my city. I often do the same and visit them in theirs. And all of us yearly make the pilgrimage back to our family home. But even when we are apart, when life is hectic and we can't physically be near each other (like during the worldwide pandemic that began in 2020), we find ways to connect with each other, sometimes over scheduled Zoom calls or by simply sending each other memes, funny pictures, life updates, jokes, book recommendations, memories, or hellos on our legendary family group chat.

We do all this, not out of obligation or because we are "supposed to," but because we actually want to. In interacting and connecting with the people who know us best, we are more able to feel love and to live more fully in our individual worlds. Somehow, in each of our hearts, there exists this magnetic pull that draws us, in the midst of a chaotic world and our own demanding lives, back to each other. It's a gentle tug toward home. Home is somewhere we can share our burdens, be celebrated, rest, laugh, and ultimately, be ourselves. When we are with each other, we are home.

I didn't realize how rare this relationship with my family was until I began noticing that many people I met didn't have this same relationship with their family. I often hear comments from friends about how they wish they had a family group chat. Colleagues voice regret that they haven't seen their family in years; others confess they haven't spoken to their families in decades. As a result, I now don't take for granted the connection I have with my family. I thank God daily that I was given a community of people who are for me, no matter what, who love the uniqueness I was created with, and even from afar, are rooting for my success in life.

Community is an intrinsic human need, one that was programmed into the very hearts of humans by God. The human longing for community is evidenced by the current lack of its presence and the negative effects that is having on individuals, what many are calling the "loneliness epidemic."[1] This is an issue that is seemingly affecting a huge number of us in the modern world, one that leaves people feeling isolated, unimportant, unseen, unloved.

Loneliness increases one's risk of depression, anxiety, and suicide, ups the likelihood of heart disease and strokes, and is even linked to premature death at levels that rival the rates of smoking and obesity.[2] Community isn't just a nice thing; it's an emotional, physical, and mental need. God created us to find ourselves and our identity in the context of relationships, where we can both be celebrated for who we are (differences and all), experience a peace that comes from the safety of loving people looking out for us, and ultimately find purpose for why we were created. And the first and most important community that we will ever have is our family.

When a child enters the world and immediately finds themselves a part of a group of people who love and support them, who celebrate them for how they were made, and give them, with all of their uniqueness, a place to belong and thrive, the child is set up for a lifetime of security and stable assurance against an insecure and chaotic world. Community is a necessary component to a whole and happy life, and God has created the family to fill that community need in a child's heart in a way nothing else ever could.

I was given the gift of a close-knit community from my family, one where I could be celebrated for who God created me to be. Traditions like Family Day and practices like family group chats are regular pictures of that reality in my life. But as I wrote this book with Mom, I began to ponder just what it was that made this closeness possible and how I can foster the same closeness in my future family.

Below are five core components I identified for building a lifegiving community within family.

1. The Unconditional Acceptance and Celebration of Each Member

Out in modern society—be it church, work, school, or friend groups—community is offered only insofar as we assimilate to the theology, tasks, interests, and style of the larger group. To fit in and be accepted into these groups, we have to change parts of ourselves lest we be denied entrance to the community we desire. The family is a place where there ought to be no requirements on acceptance into the fold. A healthy family doesn't look to "change" who each member was created by God to be, but instead embraces even vast differences into the fabric that makes up the whole of what it is. This, of course, can be difficult, trying to combine different personalities into one cohesive community; but to have a place where every member feels that they are a part of the group—no matter what—is a vital element of family cohesion.

But it doesn't stop at mere acceptance: for a child to thrive in a community, they must be more than tolerated; they must be celebrated. Creating a family culture where the uniqueness of each of its members is welcomed but also spoken of positively will be life-changing for the children within it. I knew that even though I was different from my siblings, I was accepted in my differences and even appreciated for the uniqueness I brought to our home. This gave my heart a sense of belonging and identity that ultimately gave me the confidence and support I knew I could always count on as I grew up and faced the world.

2. The Fostering of the "We"

In every great family community, there are many unique parts. But to bind them together, there must be muscles and tendons. Building the "we" of a strong family isn't so much making its members fit a mold, but instead, creating a strong foundation and a consistency of values that flows through the veins of—and is expressed by—each individual member. For our family, this was accomplished in the ways we articulated who "we" were and what "we" did:

We have fun in this family.
We think deeply in this family.
We respect each other and others in our speech and actions in this family.
We are creative in this family.
We pray together and for each other in this family.

These are less cookie-cutter molds or stringent rules, and more so guides that inform each member who the "we" is, and how the "we" looks acted out practically in community. There's a comfort in the expectation and learning of the "we" rhythms that are practiced on a day-to-day basis. And while each of these things will be expressed uniquely by the different members, there is a strong identifying factor that informs the minds of the family who they are in a real and tangible sense.

3. The Regular and Consistent Practice of Community Time and Together Moments

As we have already shared, once a year we would have Family Day. Multiple times a year we had a birthday breakfast with cinnamon rolls and went around the table and said something about the birthday boy/girl. Every Friday night we had pizza and movie nights, and every Sunday afternoon we had teatime where we would eat great food and just talk. Each of these regular practices were created, practiced, and honored with the intent of making regular spaces in time where we would build the togetherness every child needs to form strong relationships with their family.

In the act of consistently finding time to laugh, talk, eat, and rest, we formed deeper and deeper bonds, and this was done not in one moment, but thousands. This was an act that developed over decades and continues today. In choosing to make time and space for the family to gather, we were able to build our relationships and create a rich history of moments that were fostered for us to forge a closeness that never would have been possible if we had not chosen to make that time a priority and ultimately a reality.

4. The Sense of "Place" Where I Belong No Matter What

We moved many times during my upbringing. We lived in big and small houses, and even had times where we spent months traveling across the country living in hotel rooms. But no matter where we were or what house we were living in, there was a sense of sameness fostered by my mother who went to great lengths to ensure that no matter where we were living, it felt like home. This was achieved through having family dinner times, morning rituals, favorite meals, and keeping traditions. These practices gave us a strong sense of "home" and belonging and created a place we could count on to embrace us no matter what stage of life we were going through.

Seemingly simple rhythms, like my mom lighting candles, gave definition to a place we knew we belonged and could expect goodness from. So strong were these rhythms that now when I return home after a difficult season, being greeted with the sights, smells, and memories upon opening the door informs my memory, mind, and senses that I *am* home. And I am suddenly flooded with the realization that I am safe. This is something every child needs: a sense of "place" that assures them that, within its bounds, they are and will be cared for.

5. The Responsibility to Support and Love Each Other No Matter What

All of us will face difficult and trying times in our lives—times where we are weak and in need of help. Times where we are lost and in need of guidance. Times where we are poor in spirit and in need of an investment of love and care. And in these times, one of the most crucial things that can make the difference between our losing or winning the battles of life is an ever-present community that offers active and unconditional love. The family is the God-designed unit created to function as that support system and as an anchor through the storms we face. I know that no matter what I go through, I have a community of people at my back and by my side, and just knowing that allows me to walk with confidence through my story. I know this because I've experienced it multiple times throughout the most difficult trials. And it only exists because my parents fought to foster a creed of closeness, cohesion, and devotion for our entire lives.

Scripture Reading

"A new command I give you: Love one another. As I have loved you, so you must love one another. By this everyone will know that you are my disciples, if you love one another." (John 13:34–35)

FAMILY DISCUSSION QUESTIONS

1. What do you love most about your family?
2. What is the easiest and most difficult part of supporting and loving each other?

3. What is something particularly special about your family?

4. Why do you believe forming a tight community in your family is so important?

5. What are some ways you can show more support and love to your family members?

Afterword

Nathan Clarkson

Recently, my whole family gathered at our family home in Colorado. It was the first time in a long while all of us were in the same place at the same time. We four siblings are all adults now, and we each live in different places around the world—New York, Oxford, London, and sometimes Monument, Colorado—and we all pursue different callings—acting, filmmaking, writing, academics, music, and teaching. And we all have unique relationship statuses and partners: I married an actress from Los Angeles, my siblings found spouses in vastly different professions and even from different countries.

We are dressed differently—me in a T-shirt, leather jacket, and jeans; my older sister draped in a knitted sweater with a book in her hands; my older brother sporting an Oxford cloth button-down and leather shoes; and my little sister in a stylish dress and heels. But as we sprawl out on multiple couches, there exists between us a oneness, like a beautifully woven tapestry, filled with unique colors and designs that complement each other.

Somehow the diversity of our persons creates a brilliant unity that doesn't detract from the familial fabric but strengthens it. And as we sit there, it's clear that little has changed in who we are and always have been since childhood. We're bigger now, we have jobs, spouses, children, and houses of our own. But we're really who we always were. I make a snarky comment on a story my younger sister is telling about the dream she had last night, while my brother grins quietly, and my older sister is lost in the novel she's reading. And as I sit back and take in the familiar view that stretches back over decades, I suddenly feel a deep sense of peace and thankfulness at the upbringing I was given, an upbringing that gave me a place to both be celebrated for who God created me to be and a time to learn how to celebrate the ones around me for who God had created them to be.

Sometimes I think about the verse in Revelation that describes the grand procession into heaven. The author describes a beautiful vision of people from every tribe, tongue, and nation (7:9) reveling in God's glory as they walk toward eternity. I think this gives us a vision here not only for the diversity of the kingdom of God in a worldwide sense, but also the localized and beautiful uniqueness that He's created in every family—a community of individuals with every kind of mind, heart, and personality, each revealing God's glory.

Paul spoke of the church using an image of a "body" where each member was a different part of the whole. Each with their own purpose, function, ability, but each was necessary. Every family is telling a unique story with a cast of unique characters, all of whom bring life and fullness to the brilliance of the tale the family will tell and the legacy they'll leave behind. But to tell this story well, each family must accept their plot with all the ups and downs, ins and outs; they must accept the characters in it as they were cast by God with the purpose of redeeming the world. If families can capture this beautiful vision, this brilliant concept of uniqueness, they can give it not only to their children, but their children's children and future generations as well. This lasting throughline of realizing God's fullness in their life ultimately has the power to not only bring life to their individual hearts, but also bring redemption to the entire world.

Loving, accepting, and engaging with the uniqueness of your family isn't just a good method or practice, it's kingdom work that has the ability to bring God's presence on earth.

We are all fearfully and wonderfully made by the artist God who has created each of us to be completely distinctive. Understanding this amazing truth and integrating its reality into both your personal life and familial practice will be a heart-shaping and life-changing act. So, in a world that pressures, and even threatens, us and our children into conformity, thank God we know the good news of how each of us are completely, wholly, and beautifully . . . UNIQUELY YOU!

Notes

Chapter 1: Fearfully and Wonderfully Made

Epigraph: Ralph Waldo Emerson, *The Complete Works of Ralph Waldo Emerson: Essays*, 1st series (Boston & New York: Houghton Mifflin, 1903), 83.

1. Selda Koydemir, Ömer Faruk Şimşek, Tubanur Bayram Kuzgun, and Astrid Schuetz, "Feeling special, Feeling Happy: Authenticity Mediates the Relationship Between Sense of Uniqueness and Happiness," *Current Psychology* 39, no. 5 (2020): 1589–1599, https://doi.org/10.1007/s12144-018-9865-z.
2. Cindy Long, "Standardized Testing is Still Failing Students," NEA Today, March 30, 2023, https://www.nea.org/nea-today/all-news-articles/standardized-testing-still-failing-students.
3. Carl Gustav Jung, "Jung on Christianity," in *Encountering Jung*, ed. Murray Stein (Princeton, NJ: Princeton University Press, 1999), 99.

Chapter 2: Personality Types

Epigraph: C. J. Jung, *The Essential Jung*, ed. Anthony Storr (Princeton, NJ: Princeton University Press, 2013), 195.

1. Kendra Cherry, "Is Personality Genetic?," Very Well Mind, March 1, 2023, https://www.verywellmind.com/are-personality-traits-caused-by-genes-or-environment-4120707.

2. Jill Suttie, "Can Your Personality Change Over Your Lifetime?," *Greater Good Magazine*, October 15, 2018, https://greatergood .berkeley.edu/article/item/can_your_personality_change_over_ your_lifetime.

Chapter 3: Learning Styles

Epigraph: Quote by Thomas Edison in "10 Thomas Edison Quotes to Start Your School Year," Edison Innovation Foundation, Thomas Edison Muckers (blog), August 29, 2022, https://www.edisonmuckers .org/10-thomas-edison-quotes-on-education-to-start-your-school-year/.
1. Howard Gardner, *Frames of Mind* (New York City: Basic Books, 1983).
2. "Howard Gardner's Theory of Multiple Intelligences," Center for Innovative Teaching and Learning, Northern Illinois University, https://www.niu.edu/citl/resources/guides/instructional-guide/ gardners-theory-of-multiple-intelligences.shtml.
3. "Multiple Intelligences: What Does the Research Say?", Edutopia, updated July 20, 2016, https://www.edutopia.org/multiple-intelligences-research.
4. "Are Standardized Tests Reliable Indicators of Intelligence?" Infinity Learn, https://infinitylearn.com/surge/blog/general/are-standardized-tests-reliable-indicators-of-intelligence.
5. Martin V. Melosi, *Thomas A. Edison and the Modernization of America* (Glenview, IL: Scott, Foresman/Little, Brown Higher Education, 1990), 8.

Chapter 4: Big Unique Dreams

Epigraph: Christopher Reeve, "1996 Democratic National Convention Address," August 26, 1996, transcript, https://www.american rhetoric.com/speeches/christopherreeve1996dnc.htm.

1. "Creativity in Young Children," Kathy Dothage and Sara Gable, reviewers, University of Missouri, April 2022, https://extension.missouri.edu/publications/gh6041.
2. Warn. N. Lekfuangfu and Reno Odermatt, "All I Have to Do Is Dream? The Role of Aspirations in Intergenerational Mobility and Well-Being," *European Economic Review* 148 (2022): 104193, https://doi.org/10.1016/j.euroecorev.2022.104193.

Chapter 5: 5 Love Languages

Epigraph: Gary Chapman, *The 5 Love Languages* (Chicago: Northfield, 2024), 33.
1. The 5 Love Languages®, referred to generally here, include: Acts of Service, Receiving Gifts, Quality Time, Words of Affirmation, and Physical Touch. They were developed by Gary Chapman, PhD, and introduced in his book *The 5 Love Languages* from Northfield Publishing. You can learn more about the love languages at 5lovelanguages.com.
2. Selena Bunt and Zoe J. Hazelwood, "Walking the Walk, Talking the Talk: Love languages, Self-regulation, and Relationship Satisfaction," Wiley Online Library, February 24, 2017, https://onlinelibrary.wiley.com/doi/abs/10.1111/pere.12182.

Chapter 6: Heartfelt Discipline

Epigraph: Clay Clarkson, *Heartfelt Discipline: Following God's Path of Life to the Heart of Your Child* (Whole Heart Ministries, 2014), 56.
1. Malinda Wenner Moyer, "What Science Really Says About Spanking," *Scientific American*, September 1, 2016, https://www.scientificamerican.com/article/what-science-really-says-about-spanking/.

Chapter 7: Outside-the-Box Minds

Epigraph: Fred Rogers, *You Are Special: Neighborly Words of Wisdom from Mister Rogers* (New York: Penguin Books, 1995), 115.

1. "Children's Mental Health," American Psychological Association, updated May 2022, https://www.apa.org/topics/children/mental-health.
2. "Understanding Neurodiversity in Children," The Children's Guild, November 8, 2023, https://childrensguild.org/understanding-neurodiversity-in-children/.
3. Amanda Moses, "Why Has There Been a Rise in Autism and ADHD Diagnoses?" *Psychology Today*, July 14, 2023, https://www.psychology today.com/us/blog/thinking-about-becoming-a-psychologist/202307/why-has-there-been-a-rise-in-autism-and-adhd.
4. "Risk of Suicide," National Alliance on Mental Illness, https://www.nami.org/about-mental-illness/common-with-mental-illness/risk-of-suicide/.

Chapter 8: Friends and Relationships

Epigraph: Calvin, in Calvin and Hobbs (comic strip) by Bill Watterson, April 23, 1989.
1. "Youth Suicide Rates Increased During the COVID-19 Pandemic," National Institute of Mental Health, May 22, 2023, https://www.nimh.nih.gov/news/science-news/2023/youth-suicide-rates-increased-during-the-covid-19-pandemic.
2. "The Benefits of Childhood Friendships and How to Support Them," First Discoverers, https://www.firstdiscoverers.co.uk/benefits-childhood-friendships/.

Chapter 9: Lifegiving Community

Epigraph: Edith Schaeffer, *What Is a Family?* (Grand Rapids, MI: Baker Books, 1997), 39–40.
1. "New APA Poll: One in Three Americans Feels Lonely Every Week," American Psychiatric Association, January 30, 2024, https://www.psychiatry.org/news-room/news-releases/new-apa-poll-one-in-three-americans-feels-lonely-e.

2. "Loneliness and Social Isolation Linked to Serious Health Conditions Centers for Disease Control and Prevention,," April 29, 2021, https://www.cdc.gov/aging/publications/features/lonely-older-adults.html.

Sally Clarkson

AUTHOR | SPEAKER | LIFEGIVER

Over her more than four decades of marriage and ministry, Sally Clarkson has dedicated her life to faithfully discipling, mentoring, and encouraging women to live wholeheartedly for Christ and his kingdom. To learn more about her life, ministry, and messages, she invites you to join her online:

WEBSITE & BLOG | SallyClarkson.com

Choosing how to use your time wisely and well online is always a challenge as a woman, wife, and mom. If you need some spiritual encouragement, biblical inspiration and wisdom, or just some practical helps and tips, you will find all that, and more, starting here on my personal website and blog.

ONLINE COMMUNITY | LifewithSally.com

Discipleship has always been the heartbeat of my ministry. We all need personal connections with like-hearted women to help us grow. That is why I started Life with Sally, an online membership community filled with my talks and Bible studies, resources, recipes, a forum, and so much more.

PODCAST PAGE | AtHomewithSally.com

Speaking life and love into the hearts and minds of women on my weekly podcasts has been a true delight for me for the past decade. It is my way to have an intimate, homey conversation with you, and to share some personal stories and biblical lessons I've learned as a woman, wife, and mother.

Social Media
FACEBOOK | @TheRealSallyClarkson
INSTAGRAM | @Sally.Clarkson
YOUTUBE | @SallyClarkson

Whole Heart Ministries | *Keeping Faith in the Family*
ONLINE | WholeHeart.org

Whole Heart Ministries is a nonprofit Christian home and parenting ministry founded by Clay and Sally Clarkson in 1994 to give help and hope to Christian parents to raise wholehearted children for Christ.

Nathan Clarkson

ACTOR | AUTHOR | FILMMAKER | WRITER | PODCASTER

Nathan Clarkson is an award-winning actor in film and television, a Publishers Weekly bestselling author of numerous books, a Netflix trending indie filmmaker of multiple feature films, and a podcast philosopher on a multi-award winning podcast.

Online

WEBSITE | NathanClarkson.me

PODCAST | The Overthinkers

COLUMN | Cross & Culture (Patheos)

Social Media

FACEBOOK | @NathanClarkson

INSTAGRAM | @NathanJClarkson

YOUTUBE | @NathanClarkson